C000253902

DUNDEE WORTHIES

REMINISCENCES, GAMES & AMUSEMENTS

To Uncle Dave

Happy 80th Birthday

love from Colleen,

Ian, Amy Keira

B

Cavan

xxx
xx

C. ALLARDYCE & SON

SURGICAL INSTRUMENT AND APPLIANCE
MAKERS TO DUNDEE ROYAL INFIRMARY
AND OTHER LEADING INSTITUTIONS

81, Nethergate, DUNDEE

Telephone No. 2409

SPECIALISTS IN

GLOVES AND

STOCKINGS

Henry Adams & Son

"The Dundee Glovers"

6 High Street, DUNDEE

Founded in 1791   *Phone: Dundee 3775*

DUNDEE WORTHIES

WORTHIES

REMINISCENCES, GAMES
& AMUSEMENTS

Compiled by
GEORGE M. MARTIN, F.S.A. (Scot.),
31 SOUTH TAY STREET,
DUNDEE

DUNDEE UNIVERSITY PRESS
PERTH ROAD, DUNDEE
2010

This edition first published in
Great Britain in 2010
by
Dundee University Press
5th Floor Tower Building,
Perth Road, Dundee
DD1 4HN

www.dundee.ac.uk/dup

978-1-84586-115-5

First published in 1934 by
David Winter and Son, Dundee

All rights reserved

Printed in Great Britain
by Bell & Bain Ltd, Glasgow

DUNDEE   WORTHIES

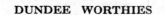

PREFACE

With a view to preserve details of the strange lives of the Worthies who eked out an existence on the streets of Dundee I have compiled the following pages. It will be obvious to the reader that many of these reminiscences would be lost by the passing of this generation.

The compiling of this work—a labour of love—was not a simple matter, as although many hundreds of elderly people were interviewed a very few could describe the peculiarities, appearance or speech of these worthies. I am grateful to all those who have given me data, especially would I thank Messrs. David Winter & Son, and Messrs. Wm. Kidd & Son, for permission to use suitable matter from their publications, Mr. John C. Willocks for liberty to make extracts from his father's book on Poet McGonagall, and Bailie Robert Blackwood for four sketches from the *City Echoes*.

I am conscious that many more biographies are to be had and if any reader will kindly send these to me at the address given below, these could be included in a subsequent edition.

The description of the games played on the open streets —now impossible with the fast traffic—is by no means complete and details or corrections would be welcomed, as would also any reminiscences of the amusements of the period covered by this book.

GEORGE M. MARTIN, F.S.A. (Scot.).

31 South Tay Street,
    Dundee.

TELEPHONE 4958

When Ordering MALT LIQUORS
ask only for those bottled by

THOMAS SMITH
THE BOTTLER

22, SOUTH LINDSAY STREET
DUNDEE

Agent for

**"VAT 69" SPECIAL LIQUEUR
YOUNGER'S (ALLOA) SPARKLING
ALES 🍺 🍺 TUBORG LAGER**

Quinnette Products Ltd.

FRUIT CRUSHES   FARNHAM
AND CORDIALS   SURREY

DUNDEE WORTHIES

Blind Hughie

" Blind Hughie " was to Dundee what " Hawkie " was to Glasgow. The one was a street singer, and the other a street wit and wag. But each in his rôle filled a place in which they gained and retained wonderful popularity, and helped to spread the fame of their respective cities, if not of themselves. Everybody knew " Blind Hughie " ; school laddies and lassies, young men and maidens, citizens generally, and by all he was regarded as a favourite. His tall, erect, portly figure, his pale, chubby, and good humoured face and frank address, and his remarkable want of pretension or assumption, contributed not a little to his reputation. His faculty of music was great, and few were more keen to gratify it. He was in ecstasy when listening to a prima donna or a master of song, and so developed and retentive was his memory, that he would with only once hearing it carry away an " air " ; then he would whistle it or croon it over to himself, and after getting the words would add the song to his budget of lyrics. His voice, from long use in the open air, was husky, rough, and cracked ; still there was music in it, and it was his fortune. Selecting a quiet spot near a street corner where crowds are always to be found, " Hughie " would take up his stand. Stretching himself erect, throwing his head well back, his walking stick hanging by the crook on his left arm, and clearing his voice he would begin his entertainment. His voice, which suffered from a peculiar back draught, as if he was short of breath, was strong and of good compass, and could be heard from a considerable distance. He entered, with the fullest sympathy, into the sentiments of his song, whether grave or gay, pastoral or patriotic, sentimental or comic, testifying his delight or enthusiasm as these feelings moved him by now and again shrugging his shoulders or jerking his arm bearing his stick. " Hughie " had a keen appreciation of humour, and appeared intensely happy when rolling off some laughable song or ballad in " broad Scotch." A favourite was " Good News "—a doggerel ditty descriptive of a ship stored with a heterogeneous mass of wares, from a needle to an anchor. The articles on sale were given in ludicrous contrast:—Razor straps and curling stanes, Epsom salts and wheelbarrows, wine grapes and tattie graips, Mason's mells and gum flowers, and coarse meal for masons. . . The list of these and such like contrasts was considerable, and being rattled off with the rapidity of rank and file musketry firing, his auditors were kept in fits of laughter.

In the course of his wanderings he visited towns in Fife and Forfar, and other districts, and was also a prominent figure at feeing markets, fairs and other gatherings. Though he was poor his honesty was true as steel, and he would have scorned to take a mean advantage of any person.

On a Saturday late at night in Arbroath, in the early autumn, when the streets were pretty dark, owing to the public lamps not having been fitted up for the winter, Hughie was rattling away in full glee at the Tower Neuk with a closely packed crowd of admirers around him. Through the crowd a poor woman squeezed her way and slipped a coin into the singer's hand. Suddenly he stopped in the middle of the verse and bawled out—" I say, mistress, that's a twa shilling piece you've gi'en me for a penny ; whaur are ye ? " " Here, Hughie ; it was me," answered the woman, " I thocht it was a penny." The honest fellow handed back the coin, and as ill luck would have it the woman hadn't a copper in her possession. Thanking Hughie, and apologising for the lack of a copper to give him, her deed of practical sympathy elicited from him—" Never mind, you'll maybe hae a penny the next time I'm here ! " The crowd laughed, and cries of " Well done, Hughie," were accompanied with a liberal shower of coppers ; an incident proving the truth of the maxim that " honesty is the best policy," and that however poor, rough, or uncouth, a street audience may sometimes appear, there is a sympathetic chord in the human breast which vibrates under the influence of a simple but noble deed.

Hugh Lennox—for such was Hughie's name—was twice married. He was also a temperate man, and by dint of providence, honesty, tact, and good luck, he maintained a tolerably respectable position, and appeared clean and tidily clothed. In the early years of his wedded life he had a comfortable little home of his own in Kirriemuir. But ere long, misfortune blighted his happiness. His wife fell into bad health, removed to Montrose, her birthplace, to be near her own people, and Hughie had to take up his abode in a common lodging-house. His wife soon afterwards died in the

Montrose Infirmary. Her funeral was grotesquely described in one of the local newspapers. It was attended by only two mourners—Hughie himself and Willie Gunn, another half-blind man who made a living by selling almanacs on the streets in winter and dealing in old books in summer. The coffin having been placed in a small, mean hearse, Hughie took hold of the vehicle at the back, and Willie linked himself into Hughie's arm. Then off the cortege started. The driver, a bit of a wag, put his horse to a trot, and the ludicrous spectacle of two blind men holding on to the rear of a hearse and laboriously running as hard as they could, created quite a scene on the streets.

In the later years of his life Hughie located himself in Dundee, and was a frequent attender at the sittings of the Police and Sheriff Courts. He fell into bad health, and died in poor circumstances about the year 1889.

Davie Begg and his Sister Tibbie

Davie and his sister lived together in a house at the west end of the town, a quarter with which they were consequently well acquainted. They were also well known to all who resided there. Both brother and sister possessed a strong begging propensity. While he endeavoured to gratify it by singing, reciting, or praying on the streets, she strolled about the Perth Road soliciting money from gentlemen, her expectation being that they would not give her anything less than silver. She was never more gleefully excited than when presented with a sixpence. Her custom was to way-lay gentlemen as they were passing, tap them on the shoulder, and say : " Gie's a sixpence ! " If there was not a ready response to the demand, she would add—" If ye're to gie's onything gie's it, because fouk'll be speaking about seeing us thegither ! " She was so importunate that the only speedy and easy way to get rid of her was to give her the coveted coin—an offer of coppers but served to increase her importunity. Her brother, Davie, boasted that he was the first preacher in St. David's Free Church. One day when the church was all but finished he happened to stroll into it to take a look round. Observing him, the workmen smiled to each other, and asked Davie " what he thought o' the kirk ? " He said " It's a grand place." " Well, Davie, now's yer chance ; gie's a sermon." And, at once, Davie ascended the stairs to the pulpit, preached in a voice so loud that made the seats

A*

dirl, and concluded his service with an eloquent prayer.
" Now," said he as he passed out, " I've opened the kirk ! "

One day he was in the Murraygate, near the Dog Well,
singing to a crowd of youngsters his favourite song of " Susie,"
when a man offered to give him a halfpenny if he would repeat
a prayer. Davie bethought himself, and said he could not
think of praying so soon after singing " Susie." The man
offered to increase his pay to a penny. Davie said he would
try it for the penny, which he received and put into his pocket.
He then reverently took off his cap, raised his eyes to heaven,
and said a most impressive prayer, the intonation being perfect,
and all the clauses arranged in proper order, embracing one
having special reference to King George and all the Royal
Family. The same prayer he had frequently repeated.

One day at Broughty Ferry, Davie was in straits for money.
Taking up a position on the street in order to conduct a
religious service, he placed his bonnet on the ground in front
of him to receive a copper from any sympathetic passer-by.
After a short pause he, with upturned eyes, began to pray
in a loud and solemn voice—" O Lord ! " then furtively
glancing at his bonnet, and discerning only a meagre coin
or two, suddenly stopped, and disdainfully exclaimed—" Is
there only fowerpence ? " and picking up his bonnet with the
coppers, slipped off to get a dram. He returned in a minute
or two and resumed the service, when he seemed charged with
great spiritual inspiration !

There is an amusing story regarding him while an inmate
of the Royal Lunatic Asylum in Albert Street. He and a
number of other inmates were occasionally visited by a philan-
thropic gentleman, who one day put a half-crown into Davie's
hand. When alone a few minutes afterwards Davie opened
his hand and observed with gleeful eyes he had received no
less than a beautiful half-crown ! " I havena'," said he,
" muckle use for you as lang as I'm here, but maybe the time
'ill come when I'll be outside thae stane dykes, and then ye'll
be handy. But whaur will I keep ye ? " was his puzzling
question ; when happening by a side glance to discern a
small hole in the wall, he slyly slipped the coin into it. " Ye
can joost bide there," he ejaculated, " till I need ye."
Unnoticed by Davie, a warder, who had observed all his
movements, resolved to play on him a practical joke. In a
day or two Davie was back at the hole in the wall, and peeping
into it to see if his half-crown was still there, he beheld, to
his painful astonishment, nothing but a miserable brown

penny. " Ugh ! " cried he in disgust, " Brownchitas ! this place is fu' o' disease ! and left the penny undisturbed. Observing at his next examination a white sixpence where he had left the penny, he bawled out—" Consumption ! " and again withdrew, leaving the coin untouched. Wondering what effect the sight of a half-sovereign would have on Davie's nerves, the warder substituted that coin for the sixpence. " Jaundice ! " roared Davie, as his eye afterwards detected the yellow coin, " but as I dinna think ye'll live lang, I'll put ye in my pooch ! " and suiting the action to the word, walked off chuckling to himself in high glee that he had derived more pleasure and profit from the joke than its humorous and ingenious perpetrator.

Jamie May

A Perth Road curiosity was Jamie May, a silly harmless creature, whom the boys delighted to tease, meanwhile bawling :

> " Jamie, Jamie May,
> His mither had to watch him
> Workin' on the railway."

On summer evenings it was then the custom for lads and lasses to go together to the church, or enjoy a walk out the Perth Road. To see them gave Jamie intense delight. This simple pastime was more to him than perhaps a costly entertainment in the theatre or concert hall patronised by richer persons. He would stand for hours at a certain corner and see the prettily dressed maidens with their beaux pass by ; and seemed so charmed with the sight that he appeared transfixed to the spot, and the happy smile that continually lit up his features testified how exquisite was the pleasure that was his. He felt proud of them, talked gleefully about them ; and living in poverty, week in, week out, he found the dreary monotony of his days, unrelieved by anything else to cheer, amply compensated for by the joy he derived from the kaleidoscopic moving crowds on the Sunday evenings.

Andrew Body

A simple harmless man, meanly clad, about fifty years of age, tried to earn a living by turning " cat-ma " or a somersault on the pavement, to amuse any who might be generously inclined to hand him a copper.

" Gie's ane o' yer best anes, Andrew," some teasing boy
would say, " an I'll gie ye a ha'penny." The acrobatic feat
was no sooner asked for than it was performed. When he
first began these street performances some mean people
withheld the halfpenny from the poor man after he had earned
it. But this dishonesty Andrew ever afterwards prevented
by making sure the halfpenny was in his hand before he would
give a specimen of his acrobatic skill. And to the honour
of the harmless creature be it said, he never once proved
dishonest to those who prepaid him for amusing them.

" Daft Jamie "

Another of " Old Dundee's " characters was " Daft Jamie."
He was intensely fascinated by " bonnie things," as he called
them, such as little bits of shining glass or pebbles, a large
collection of which he carried about in his pockets. The boys
knew him well, and found great fun in inviting him to show
them his curiosities, which he at once exhibited with an
ecstasy of delight. On one occasion a reputedly " daft man,"
from Perth, came into Jamie's way, when the latter, eyeing
him with a look of keen jealousy hailed him with : " What
are ye doin' here, there's plenty o' daft fouk here without
ye ! "

" Queen Anne,"

who resided in the Nethergate, was known for a weakness
which revealed itself in a love for decorating herself with
little bits of coloured silk ribbons and lace, tinselry and trinkets.
Nothing pleased her better than to be presented with trifles
such as these, which she would there and then pin to her
dress, and walk away showing them off with a variety of
gestures and courtly airs, saying in a kind of sing-song—
" I'm Queen Anne."

" Waterloo,"

an old man, of short stature, and who wore a Tam o' Shanter
bonnet, was another striking character. The nickname was
given to him by the boys as his silliness found vent in what
he termed his " Rehearsal of the Battle of Waterloo." The
offer of a halfpenny was sufficient to induce him to give a
representation of how the British soldiers fought in the
memorable struggle. His stick did duty as a sword, which
he wielded fast and furiously, and woe to anybody who might

happen to come within its sweep while he was slaying the imaginary enemy !

" Jeely fit " . . . " Coo heel " . . . " Tirr."

Such were the nicknames boys bawled out when they hailed " Willie " Morris, the trustworthy messenger of Mrs. Gibb, flesher in Crichton Street, while on his way with a large basket filled with parcels of beef to deliver to her customers. The boys so greatly annoyed him that he would suddenly turn round on them, chase them a few yards, and howl— " Boo, boo ! " One day, Dean Horsley—a fine looking, burly man—(son of the great Bishop Horsley) at whose house Willie regularly delivered a parcel, was walking along the Nethergate to the centre of the town, when he descried Willie surrounded by a crowd of his usual tormentors, who were uttering deafening cries of " Coo heel ! " " Jeely fit ! " " Tirr ! " The Dean, interfering on Willie's behalf, said : " Oh, boys, you young rascals, go back and do not disturb the poor man." At this reproof the boys fled ; and to the inquiry of a friend, " What's this, Dean ? " the Dean explained —" A simple man, Willie here, who delivers meat, a good-natured useful creature, is greatly annoyed by these boys ; they don't mean any harm, but they put the poor man very much about." Willie was for many years Mrs. Gibb's faithful messenger, and latterly the boys entirely ceased their molestations.

To the Rev. James Johnston, or " Ranter Johnson," as he was familiarly known, Willie was warmly attached, and was a regular attender at his prayer meeting during the week. The meeting-house was at that time at the west end of Baltic Street, and was reached by a wooden stair. The devotional exercises were conducted by the " Ranter," the congregation meanwhile reverently kneeling. Willie was one of the most devout, his interjected exclamations—" Amen ! " " Lord do so ! " being so loud that they could easily be heard by any persons passing along the street. Latterly, the world began to go ill with Willie. The infirmities of age rendered him unfit for his occupation, and brought him face to face with abject poverty. Silly as he had been regarded, the spirit of sturdy Scotch independence strongly lived in his breast. Though no longer able to carry heavy parcels as a shop messenger, he determined to apply the reduced strength he still possessed in selling " camstane," and thus try to earn

NATIONAL HEALTH INSURANCE OPTICIANS

GLASSES !

Glasses indicate good sense rather than bad sight, and with the elegance of modern eye wear, appearance does not suffer in the least. There is no need to permit dangerous conditions of the eyes any longer. Consult us. Appointments can be arranged to suit your convenience.

D. M^cINNES

Ophthalmic Optician

Refractionist
A. D. Kinnoch
F.B.O.A.

4 So. Lindsay St.

DUNDEE

Refractionist
C. C. A. Scott
F.S.M.C.

KODAK DEALERS   II   ALL PHOTO. SUPPLIES

FOOT COMFORT

*W*E are continually meeting men who tell us of the comfort they get from wearing our shoes. This is not chance. Our careful selection from a variety of widths makes it possible to fit the narrowest and widest feet correctly, giving comfort where "mass production" methods cannot. Our prices are moderate, and the quality has made a standard by which other shoes are judged.

A. POTTER & SON

For Fitting Footwear

Murraygate   Dundee

a livelihood, even though he knew it would be difficult and precarious. With his basket containing " cam " on his arm, as he walked along the street, and from door to door, he appeared a lank, long, stooping figure, moving with an infirm feeble step, which gave him the air of being older than he was. Good old man ! he is yet visible to my mind's eye ; lean, wrinkled, shabby, poor, slow of speech, and of ungainly aspect ; yet, from his inoffensive nature and the admirable qualities of his soul, excelling those of many blessed with riches, he was pleasant to look at in spite of his rags, ugliness, age, and poverty.

After his death, a Waxwork Company, whose exhibition was then occupying the Thistle Hall, produced a truthful wax likeness of Willie ; and, having purchased the clothes he had worn and the veritable basket in which he had hawked his " camstane," these were used in attiring and equipping the figure which represented Willie in the attitude in which he had long been seen in the streets.

John Fergusson, or " Pie Jock "

There was no better known character in Dundee than " Pie Jock," whose memory now lives in only a comparatively few Dundonians. He was at first a heckler, then he hawked flagons, coffee-pots, pans and jugs, and after that pies on every week night. Some of the oldest retain vivid recollections of his familiar figure as he trudged along the streets with his smoking pie-oven slung by a leather strap over his shoulder. The pies were made by Mr. Peebles, a baker, whose shop, in the Perth Road, was almost directly opposite to that presently occupied by Mr. Neave, baker. They were in great favour, and, to push their sale, Mr. Peebles hired " Pie Jock " to act as itinerating agent, a duty which he performed with great fidelity. When the oven had been filled with steaming hot pies, and a fire lighted under it to keep them warm, Jock left the shop with his burden, which in size and form pretty much resembled a barrel organ. As soon as he started on his way towards the centre of the town his cry " Pies, Hot Pies ! " attracted groups of lads and lasses who largely patronised him. Pies were not so rife then as they are now, and " siller " was not so rife either, the wages of a vast number of working people not exceeding 6s. or 7s. a week. " There were not many fine things in those days," said an elderly lady to me, whom I interviewed with the view of obtaining reminiscences of the pie-vendor, and a tuppenny pie from " Pie Jock " on a Saturday night was regarded as a great luxury. His figure was light, short and crooked, and bent to one side ; his clothes were thread-bare, having rents stitched, and holes patched, and a light cloth cap, drawn down over his eyes, covered his towsey locks.

In his later days, when the pie trade embraced many competitors, the demand for his pies so rapidly declined that Mr. Peebles discontinued " Pie Jock's " services, and the latter then endeavoured to earn a living, very poor at the best, by hawking laces and other small wares which he carried in a basket. On the Saturday nights he hawked the *Police Gazette*, which was printed and published by a Mr. Brown in the Scouringburn. The paper bore on one side printed reports of the cases that had been tried during the week in the Police Court, and Jock would remain on the High Street all Saturday night up to the latest hour, peregrinating through the seething crowds, and crying—" P'lice Gazeet ; this week ! Great crimes th' day, an' a' Irish ! " On the following Saturday his cry would perhaps be different, such as " P'lice Gazeet, this week ; great crimes ; the Scotch as bad's the Irish." A libellous attack on a public official killed the *Gazette*, and " Jock," ceasing as its itinerating agent, added match-paper, blacking, and blue to his stock of small household articles. Boys in their roystering fun annoyed him very much, stealthily tugging at his basket, jostling against him, and crying " Pie Jock ; Pie Jock ! " and sometimes singing :

> " Pie Jock beats them a',
>   For he's been up and round the moon
> Wi' John o' Arnha."

The harmless creature was often so provoked that he would suddenly turn round upon his assailants and chase them, meanwhile also threatening to beat them with his stick.

On the sad day when intelligence was received of the death of Prince Albert, Jock was seen walking in the Wellgate, very solemnly, with white muslin wound round his hat, and falling in long streamers down his back to his heels. Asked the meaning of the display, he answered—" Mourning for Prince Albert." Jock, who was never married, lived alone in a house in Ritchie's Lane, in which he was found dead on Thursday, July 9, 1863. He had attained the advanced age of 70 years.

Another Pie Jock

Pie Jock in his earlier days was employed for a short time by a Hilltown cowfeeder to carry milk. Jock's customers resided mostly in the Ferry Road and Blackscroft and it was his practice to commence supplying the furthest east customers first. One eventual morning he forgot to water his milk, and it was only when he reached the door of his first customer that the sad omission flashed on his wounded feelings.

A large tub of fine clear water stood by the door and thrice did Jock dilute his milk with a tankard from the tub before the maid came with the jugs. Jock served her and went on, but whilst at the door of his next customer she beckoned him to return. Jock returned and was ushered into the parlour where sat the master who had tasted the milk. "John," said he, "I should feel obliged if you could henceforth supply the milk and the water separately, and allow me the pleasure of mixing them myself." "Weel, weel, sir, it's useless to tell a lie about it, for I suppose, sir, you watched me when . . ." "No, no, John, but the fact is that the children bathe at home and the tub at the door was full of sea water, John."

"Match Paper" Willie

was a stout elderly man who, on Saturday nights, hawked match-paper on the High Street, and, in November and December, almanacs "for the incomin' year." His match-paper, made up in pennyworths, he carried in a bunch under one arm, while he helped himself along by means of a crutch. "Match-pipp—ar; match-pipp—ar," uttered intermittently in a strong, but harsh voice, could be heard above the din all over the High Street; and as, at that time, there were no lucifer matches—a smoker having to use a flint and a steel and a bit of match-paper to get a light for his pipe— Willie had many patrons, whose personal testimony was that his match-paper was uncommonly good. Occasionally, in moving about the street, he would sing the following verses of doggerel to attract attention :

> "Ye lasses far and near,
>   Come listen to my sang ;
> Ye'll maybe think its queer,
>   But I'll no detain ye lang."
> Wi' ye're bonnets, braid, p'lice, and plaid,
>   An' curls hangin' pretty.

              Yer flooers neatly laid,
                 Oh, I canna say but weel they set ye."
Chorus :   " Whack rowdy, Row-dow, fal de ral, de ray."

   This was immediately followed by the cry : " Match-pipp—ar," and of course by the sale of a good few penny bunches of the pipe lighter.

A Cow with a Literary Taste

   In the early days of the *Courier*, that paper was delivered on the morning of publication, which occurred once a week, at the houses of the subscribers. This duty was performed by the younger apprentices, after they had worked all the previous day and night, and when, of course, they were much in need of rest and sleep. The town was divided into districts and a district was assigned to each apprentice. The length of the journey may be imagined from the fact that leaving the office with their bundles of papers about six it was about nine o'clock ere they reached their own homes. In the eastern district a *Courier* had to be delivered at the Dundee Parish Manse, which was situated in the Ferry Road and to the South of Lilybank Road. The glebe, a large field of twenty or thirty acres, lay between these roads, and, when it was in grass, the printer lad generally made a near " cut " through it from Lily-bank Road to the Manse.

   On a warm summer morning, and when about half way over the glebe, he was tempted to lie down on the grass to rest for a few minutes, placing at his side the *Courier* intended for Mr. M'Lauchlan, the parish minister. Tired and drowsy he, in the warm sunshine, quickly fell soundly asleep. Utterly unconscious of duty and all nature around him, he became an interesting and attractive object to the minister's cow grazing not far from the spot. With " stately step and slow," and with head extended, crummie walked in a direct line to him, made a few sniffs, and becoming fascinated by the scent of the newly printed paper, instantly began to devour it. The noise of this operation wakened the lad, who was horrified to see his paper disappearing down crummie's throat. What was he to do ? He had not another *Courier* left. There was no alternative but to walk back all the way to the *Courier* Office in Key's Close, Nethergate, and appeal for another paper for the minister, or go to the minister and make a plaintive explanation of all that had happened. But at this juncture Mr. M'Lauchlan, who had been an amused observer of the scene from the Manse window, made his appearance ; and consoled the weeping lad by saying not to grieve about the loss of the paper as he would soon get another, and humorously added : " I have often heard it questioned whether the public of Dundee had any literary taste, but, after what I have just seen with my own eyes, there cannot be the least doubt about the literary taste of the parish minister's cow ! "

Rev. Dr. Archibald Watson

The Doctor, who was minister of the parish of Dundee, was an eloquent and popular preacher, and an ardent promoter of church extension.

The highest honour the Established Church could bestow was conferred on him by his election to the Moderatorship of the General Assembly. A valued factor in the public life of the city generally, he was several years chairman of the School Board, and was a useful member of the Free Library Committee. His talent and tact, his rare intelligence, and ever present sagacity, rendered inestimable service in every duty he undertook. He had a quaint power of humour too, humour of the kind we call pawky.

A few years before he died, Dr. Watson was appointed one of the Queen's chaplains, and occasionally preached before her late Majesty at Balmoral. On the first of these occasions, he was, on his return to Dundee, interviewed by the late Mr. James Peddie, well-known as editor, reporter and newspaper man generally, and the following colloquy is said to have occurred :

Mr. P.—" Now, Doctor, I am anxious to know how the Queen received you—what she said to you ; not for publication, you know, but just for my own information ? "

Dr. W.—" You're sure it's not for publication ? "

Mr. P.—" Certainly not. I give you my word."

Dr. W.—" Well, she just said : ' How's Peddie ? ' "

Harry Kail

Sandy Cameron, one of nature's daft wyllies, acquired the above cognomen from the following ludicrous circumstance : The kail-pat had been frequently plundered of the solid part of its contents, ere it was considered ready for family use, and Sandy, who was really guilty, was blamed for the theft. In order to shift the blame to another party he one day seized upon " puir pussy " (an excellent thief, no doubt, in most cases, though innocent in this), lifted the pat lid, and thrust her in amongst the kail, carefully holding down the cover till the poor, unfortunate animal was quiet enough. On his mother's return, he removed the cover, exclaiming : " See, mither—just look here ! I was blamed for stealin' the beef, but dere's the thief ! " at the same time pulling out " puir pussy's " carcase.

Another version

This was a droll character, known by the sobriquet of " Hairy Kail." His real name was " Sandy " Cameron, and he resided in Fish Street. He was a little silly, went about with his shirt front open, exposing his breast, and tried to earn a little by selling small wares. In endeavouring to dispose of these he quickly lost control of his temper, when any housewife curtly refused to buy. " I don't require anything ! " sharply exclaimed a woman on opening the door in response to his knock, and then clashed the door in his face. " Don't require ! don't require ! " frequently shouted the irate vendor, as he withdrew and descended the stair to the street. He often went to the harbour, and was generally present at the Edinburgh landing slip, where passenger steamers sailed or arrived, to pick up a copper or two by begging. It is said his nickname " Hairy Kail " was originated by an extraordinary incident. One day when his mother had gone out on a message she left the kail pot on the fire, having previously put the requisite ingredients, including a piece of beef, into the pot. " Hairy," who was left in charge of the house removed the beef, plunged the cat into the pot, and held the lid firmly down until the animal was boiled to death. When his mother returned he was full of glee, and greeted her with the exclamation—" Hairy kail the day, mither ; hairy kail the day."

Daft Wisdom

Daft Jock Imrie, who was well known in this locality, happening " once upon a time " to pass a grocer's shop in the Murraygate, saw an uncovered quantity of oil standing in a conspicuous place close by the door. Jock stepped in apparently on business, and, having a pair of shoes in his hand which stood much in want of greasing, dropped them intentionally amongst the fat of the whale. On lifting out his shoes,

Jock swore lustily at the shopkeeper for keeping " things sae muckle in the way ! "

Geordie Mill

Geordie was the gravedigger of the Howff over 100 years ago. He was also the minister's man of the Steeple Kirk. His stature was much below the average, but he made up for it in girth.

One day he was busy " howkin' in a six-fit layer," when some of the little boys playing about the meadowside stole into the Howff and stole the ladder which he used for climbing out of and into the grave. The minister was in the habit of leaving the manse every forenoon, walking through the orchard where Bank Street now is, and promenading up and down the path between the gravestones, conning over his sermon for the Sabbath. Hearing a most unusual rumbling sound close at hand he proceeded to investigate and he soon discovered Geordie, who was prancing up and down the " six fit " foaming at the mouth, and using fearful language. The clayey sides of the grave were all clawed and " scartet " where Geordie had been making frantic but ineffectual attempts to get out. The minister was appalled at his beadle's profanity, and looking down, he cried out " Geordie Mill, I'm mair than astonished to hear a man in your poseeshun an' wha has sut unner me for mair than forty years, cursin' and swearin' an' usin' langidge o' that description. Repent Geordie Mill, repent afore it's ower late." Geordie gulped down some fiery expletives and shaking his fist he yelled up to the minister " Repentance, be ——. Hoo' often hiv' I heard ye preachin' there's nae repentance in the grave ! "

Geordie was accused of being in league with Edinburgh professors for the purpose of supplying them with bodies for dissection and a Mr. Wm. McNab, who was born in Forfar in 1789, was a weaver to trade and was appointed presentor in the East church, stayed next door to Geordie and is thought to have guessed pretty well the reason for Geordie's " fu pooch." Along with others he used to keep watch on the sexton and the Old Howff, but failed to catch the resurrectionists red-handed.

One night, however, the watchers espied and chased a lad named McInally. One of the men in pursuit thrust a sword into the fugitive when it broke, and half of it is said to be preserved in the Dundee Museum.

FRESH  *FISH.*

Large Selections of all kinds of Fresh and Cured Fish
Daily Supplies   -:-   Moderate Prices

JAMES   S.   YOUNG,

Fish, Rabbit, Poultry & Game Merchant,

250 HILLTOWN,   **67 WELLGATE,**
'Phone 4903   **DUNDEE**   'Phone 6460

Specialties :—

FILLETED HADDOCKS, - LINE COD FILLETS, - FILLETED LEMON SOLES,
PRIME COD,   -   LINE LING,   -   LOCAL EGGS AND TRAPPED RABBITS

Expert Filleters   -:-   Smart Service
Orders Called for and Promptly Delivered
-:- Hotels and Restaurants Catered For -:-

SELECTED *FISH*

MISS B. THOMSON

(Sole Partner: JAMES S. YOUNG),

𝔉𝔦𝔰𝔥 𝔐𝔢𝔯𝔠𝔥𝔞𝔫𝔱

23 NETHERGATE, DUNDEE

Telephone No. 3235

Daily Deliveries to all parts of the City and Suburbs,
Orders going by Post, Train or Bus, receive Careful
-:-   :-:   and Prompt Attention   -:-   -:-

FINEST *QUALITY*

The following are two poems written by Mr. McNab.

The Roond Moo'ed Spade

An' if the tale that's tauld be true
A greater gain he has in view,
Which mak's his fryin' pan richt foo'
    To skirl baith nicht an' mornin'.

Geordie Mill wi' his roond moo'ed spade
Is wishin' aye for mair fouk deid,
For the sake o' the donnal an' the bit shortbread,
    When he gangs wi' the spaiks i' the mornin'.

A porter cam' to Geordie's door,
A hairy trunk on his back he bore,
Which the Quentin' Durward frae Leith shore,
    Brought roond that very mornin'.

This trunk, I'm tauld, contained a line
Wi' sovereigns to the amount o' nine,
The price o' a weel-fed sonsie quine,
    They had sent to Munro ae mornin'.

But Geordie to conceal their plan,
A story tauld as false as lang,
Sayin' the trunk belonged to a travellin' man,
    That wad call for it next mornin'.

Noo Geordie doon to Robbie goes,
The doctor's line to him he shows,
Which wished frae them a double dose,
    By the coach on Wednesday mornin'.

Says Robbie, " Is the box come back ? "
" Oh, yes," says Geordie, giein' the purse a shak',
" An' we maun gae an' no' be slack
    To fill't again ere mornin'."

Quo' Robbie's wife ; " Oh, sirs, tak tent,
For sure a warnin' I've been sent,
Which tells me ye will yet repent
    Yer conduct on some mornin'."

" Ye fool," quo' Robbie, " hush yer fears,
While I've the keys fat deil can steer's ?
We've been weel paid for't ten past years,
    Think o' auchteen pounds i' the mornin'."

Sae aff they set to Tam an' Jock,
The lads that used the spade and pock,
An' wi' Glenarf their throats did soak
 To keep them brisk till mornin'.

The hour grew late, the tryst was lain
Amang these Resurrection men,
When each his glass did freely drain,
 Sayin', " Here's success to the mornin'."

But Robbie noo does sair repent,
His slightin' o' the warnin' sent,
For the noise o' a second coffin's rent
 Caused in Dundee a deil o' a mornin'.

A Lamentation for the Loss o' The Roond Moo'ed Spade

Oh Ann, dear wife, sair noo I mourn,
To see our fortunes backward turn,
Wi' grief tears rin like a burn,
 For want o' my guid spade.

An' noo there's naething left for me
But thae four stoops o' misery,
An' weavin' at this low degree
 A sad, sad change, indeed.

As lang's I used the roond moo'ed tool,
We neither wanted meat nor fuel,
Nor yet a drink oor hearts to cool,
 When e'er they stood in need.

But he wha leads the auld kirk ban'
Has heard the skirl o' oor pan,
An' filled the toon fu' o' a sang,
 That's dwined me o' my spade.

Aye, Geordie, sair it gars me greet,
To hear your name sung on the street,
An' see oor neebours' smiling cheek,
 When e'er they hear or see't.

I was doon at Yeuchan Dora's door,
Last night, a mob, I'm sure twa score,
Your " Roond Moo'ed Spade " did yalp an' roar,
 Till't almost rave my head.

Oh, aye oor neebours hae made jeer,
Wi' that cursed sang 'bout new year,
An' happy still they'll be to hear,
　　That I maun weave for bread.

An' there's that tattie monger loon,
Wha's been sae rash to fill my room
Tho' wi' a rung I'd crack his croon,
　　Shair sma' mane wad be made.

Nae mair in leather coats he'll deal,
In pecks an' lippies nor hale sale,
But troke the lang whites 'neath the feal,
　　A kind that's better paid.

An' they baith frast an' rime can thole,
At noon they'll plant, at night they'll hole,
An' sell at auchteen pound the boll,
　　When sent to college head.

But had I kent in days o' yore,
For ane I'd sent, I'd sent a score,
An' laid the gowdens up in store,
　　To help this time o' need.

But oh, if my guid freen', Munro,
Wad now on me some peety show,
To try, I'll tak' my stock an' go,
　　Sae fareweel to my spade.

Jimmie and Leebie Threedie

About fifty years ago Jimmie Alexander was employed in one of the three rope works situated between the Perth Road and Magdalene Green and many remember the tall, very lanky man footing his way between the rope works and his house in Milnbank Road. No other pedestrian could keep pace with Jimmie who had almost four feet of a stride and a natural swing which carried him forward at a tremendous rate. The older generation will confidently tell you that modern hikers wouldn't have had a look-in with Jimmie. In his youth Jimmie had only two hobbies—his work and long walks in the country. Naturally, exercise of this healthy description kept away superfluous flesh, and to his friends he was known as the " Threed " hence the name " Jimmie Threedie." Later in life Jimmie developed a thirst and the " young bloods " of Lochee provided the money

to see Jimmie drink twelve bottles of Ballingall's Tuppenny
at a sitting and gradually Jimmie sank lower and lower
until he became a nuisance and particularly so to his sister
Leebie, who had been to him a mother and sister. In the
last few years of his life, Jimmie retained his walking ability
but with a haunted look he was continuously looking over
his shoulder as if followed by some sinister ogre and kept
muttering to himself some unintelligible language. Leebie,
a God-fearing woman, was sorely tried by her erring brother
and many a hard earned shilling was stolen from her by Jimmie.
Leebie tried to save her brother from the paths of iniquity
by asking him to think of his soul and received the irreverent
rejoinder ; " I've mair interest in the sole of ma' buik."
She was a regular attender at the Parish Church services
and a most attentive listener.

Only when her wardrobe was shabby did Leebie abstain
from worshipping under the Rev. Wm. Wright and when
a benefactress gave her cast-offs, a gleam of happiness came
to Leebie's eyes and she again, bible in hand, communed
with others in the House of God. In her later days she resided
in " Bible Row " a name given to a row of houses now
demolished, the name either having been derived from the
fact of there having been one of the earliest churches in
Lochee erected on the site or from the religious propensities
of the tenants. A correspondent sent the writer the following
touching little episode.

A knock came to the door of his home and he being at
hand he saw the poor old soul. " Mother, here's Leebie
Threedie." To which his mother replied, " Miss Alexander,
if you please," in a corrective and dignified manner. My
correspondent never forgot the lesson. Leebie had many
good friends and when the purse permitted she journeyed
round with her basket of smallwares and at other times
earned an honest copper by singing Christian hymns in the
street. Hers was a drab life, a lesson in devotion to all
who knew her, and now, having reached The Haven no doubt
she has received the " Well done good and faithful servant."

Donal—the Drover. Coo-heel

A quaint character who regularly frequented the Cattle
Market over forty years ago. A tall lanky man with a very
prominent nose and stubbly beard and garmented in the
cast-offs of the farmers who took an interest in him. Every

Tuesday and Friday Donal appeared early and greeted the market visitors with cap in hand " If you please, a penny to buy bread." At the conclusion of the sales Donal picked up odd jobs herding the cattle to the railway stations and in some cases to farms many miles away from the sale ring. On one occasion Donal got a herd to take to a farm near Forfar over 14 miles away and on his return to the market he was asked by his confreres how he had got on.

Donal replied : " Rotten ! Scurvy beggar. He gae me a tanner (6d.) but I got the better o' him. I sleepit in his field a' nicht wi-out tellin' him."

Poor Donal was the butt of the urchins both male and female with frequent " Coo-heel, Coo-heel ! "

Sandy Robb

An old man who had seen service with the " Kilties" and on pension pay days invariably made visits to the " Taverns in the Town." When in the first stages of jollity he would recite with dramatic fervour " The Charge of the Light Brigade," but in the succeeding stages would endeavour to clear the streets with his dangerous stick. In his later days Sandy became a pusher of the Sandwich Board on two wheels and when the young bloods took possession of the after part of the waggon, Sandy thought it his duty to stay between the trams and be whirled round and round the street until relieved on the appearance of the " Limb' of the Law."

Dundee's Smallest Citizen

The familiar figure of William Mallachan, better known as Tommy Dodds, will be seen no more in the streets of Dundee.

Tommy died in the Eastern Hospital in 1930. He was in his 72nd year.

Tommy's claim to public attention was based on the fact that nature had been unkind to him in the matter of stature.

He was only 49 inches in height, and was probably Dundee's shortest citizen ; but, despite his little bulk, he was " guid gear," alert and independent in mind, and gifted with a glib tongue which made him conqueror in many a battle of wits. With all sections of the community Tommy was a favourite.

He was a native of Dundee, and spent his whole life in the city.

So far as employment was concerned, he had a varied career. For many years he was with different boot emporiums as outdoor " shopwalker " and messenger.

Later he was engaged on the pleasure steamer *Cleopatra*, and for a good number of years back he was a cheery little pedlar, vending his wares from a basket in all parts of the city.

" The strongest bootlaces ever made " were his speciality.

Had he cared, Tommy, in his younger days, might have been on the music-hall stage. He had repeated offers to join " turns " which required a comical dwarf but he always turned them down.

With great gusto he used to tell of a fistic encounter he had in Castle Street with a dwarf remarkably like himself, not only in height, but in physical features.

The other dwarf was a member of an acrobatic quartette which was fulfilling a week's engagement at the People's Palace. Encountering Tommy in Castle Street, he seemed greatly interested in the likeness and stared at him.

The Dundee midget was perhaps a little rude to his fellow Lilliputian. " What are ye lookin' at ? " said Tommy in that indignant tone which he could effectively employ, and the query immediately brought out a fighting challenge from the stranger.

According to Tommy's version of the affair, he immediately went for his man. The bout was witnessed by a big crowd convulsed with laughter. Even the policemen saw the humour of it and did not separate the combatants.

Also according to Tommy, he was an easy winner, although it must be confessed that he got the verdict by " giving the head " to his opponent.

Tommy had a fondness for the police.

It was his proud boast that he frequently assisted the officers on the Overgate beat when he was employed in that neighbourhood. He carried a policeman's whistle, and when trouble arose in the street a sly blast from Tommy often worked wonders.

Before the state of his health necessitated his removal to the Eastern Hospital he lived in Seagate, and when he celebrated his 70th birthday a number of his friends in the district suitably marked the event. He was entertained in the saloon of Mr. T. W. Campbell, hairdresser, Gellatly Street, and presented with a number of gifts.

Tommy had many ways of earning an honest " copper "

amongst which was the lifting up with his mouth of coins laid on the floor or pavement, without bending his knees, but the most lucrative was collected by the bar tenders of public houses in the vicinity of Tommy's occupation.

Tommy was frequently importuned to join in the " drinks " with sympathetic admirers, but resolutely refused, he being a life-long abstainer, but made as an excuse to joining the convivial party his strict attention to business and remarked " if the well-wisher would leave the price of the refreshment with the bar-tender, I'll get it efter " which he did in the coin of the realm.

Bobby Clement and Mag Gow (Moochin' Mag)

Bobby, diminutive in size, was a tailor by trade and was troubled with a big thirst, which offence brought him to the cells in West Bell Street with which his female partner was also well acquainted, and both found themselves engaged behind prison bars, where they, on account of good work were well treated. Bob used his needle and Mag did the washing and scrubbing.

One day, walking down Bucklemaker Wynd (now Victoria Road), Bobby met an inspector of the police and asked him if it were possible to steal anything out of prison. To which question came the reply : " No Bobby, you couldn't do that." Bobby opened his jacket and bade the Inspector look at his new vest made of similar cloth to that worn by the " limb of the law." The Inspector gave Bobby a pat on the head and remarked " you're a clever wee fellow."

Blue Jock

A harmless, cheery but dirtily clad old man, who walked with a peculiar hobble. The ordinary pedestrian would have imagined that Jock never saw water from one year's end to the other but he was an expert swimmer and often took boys down to the Stannergate and taught them the useful art. He would take a boy, and sometimes two, on his back and when away from the shore would topple them off. If they could reach the shore safely " All's well " but Jock always made sure of a rescue. Had he lived in Burns' time he would have been worthy of a place in the Jolly Beggars. He used to entertain the admiring youngsters with a more or less musical jingle about the fall of the Tay bridge (28th December, 1879) which had just recently occurred.

" The Tay Brig's broken, I'm come to mend it ;
Fal the diddle di do ! Fal the diddle day.
How shall I get over ?
The ducks and the geese, they all swim over ;
Fal the diddle di do ! Fal the diddle day."

Geordie—the Policeman

One of the old school of policemen who efficiently did their duty on the streets of Dundee 50 years ago, and who was always more anxious to prevent crime than be accessory to making it.

Geordie had humorous ways of expressing himself by authoritative waving of his hands, straightening himself up as became a " limb of the law," and as the following stories will tell, made many a *lapsus linguæ*.

Before doing so, however, it is necessary to inform the reader that in these days a policeman was given various names, among others, these names were : " A Peeler," " A " Bobbie," " A Snout," " A Poo-it," or " A Slop." The derivation of the first two appellations comes from Sir Robert Peel who reorganised the old constabulary, " Snout " no doubt by the policeman poking his " nose " sometimes where it was not wanted, but the compiler has failed to find a reason for the word " Slop." In this article on Geordie—the police-man will be called the " Bobbie."

The "Bobbie " had made a capture and was marching his victim down to the Nick (jail) when the culprit made a pathetic appeal :

" Hey, Geordie, wait till I run ower to the shoppie for a bit o' 'baccy."

Geordie : " D—— a fear. I'm no daft, dae ye think I'd trust ye to come back. Na ! na ! you stand there and I'll gang."

An entertainment was being given in a large hall and as the majority of the audience were young lads and lasses having their likes and dislikes in regard to the quality of the entertainments or the ability of the artists, they showed their approval or disapproval in a boisterous manner, so much so, that the management sought the soothing influence of the " Bobbie." With martial step in he came, and with an important air walked down the passageway. Stillness restored, he shouted : " Come on noo' lads and lasses, it's no outside yer in."

The residents in a narrow street were pestered by youngsters of both sexes playing " fitba " and doing considerable damage to windows, doors, etc. One day it got so uproarious that the " Bobbie " was called and naturally before his arrival the players had decamped. The complainer was interrogated by the " Bobbie " in the following manner.

" Whit kind of laddies were they, Mrs. Perky ? "

" Oo', aye ! Yes ! Yes ! jist ordinar' laddies."

" Phat were they playin' wi' ? "

" Aye ! Aye ! a ' baw.' "

" Wist a round one ? "

To allow pedestrians to have a clear passage on the pavement one of the duties of the " Bobbie " is to move from the wall edge all loungers, to the kerb. Geordie appears at one of the regular stances of the street debaters and lectures them on the frequency of their breaking the law and threatening them with the penalties thereof. One of the ringleaders remarked " That's richt Geordie, get a ' Bobbie ' tae them."

An accident had taken place in a busy thoroughfare and as usual a large crowd congregated.

Along comes the " Bobbie " with measured and important step. Pushing his way through the crowd he sees the carter in comparative pain.

" I had an accident, ' Bobbie.' "

" Aye ! Aye ! What's yer name and address and whar dae ye work ? "

" Aye ! Aye ! Well-a-well ! Noo tell me the truth, were ye on the lorry when ye fell off ? "

A class known as the " corner boys " were a nuisance to pedestrians, but more particularly to the " Bobbie " on the beat. This class was common in all the streets, shouting, arguing, spitting, taking liberties with passers-by, etc., when the " Bobbie " making them shift from the pavement remarked : " Come awa' noo lads, if everybody stands there how can ither folks get past."

After a most enjoyable game the wee laddies, as was quite common, had the misfortune to do a small damage and for which they were rounded up before the " Bobbie." According to regulations a note-book is produced and full particulars of the damage entered therein. With authority the " Bobbie " takes the names and addresses of the accused.

Proceeding with his duty he asked :

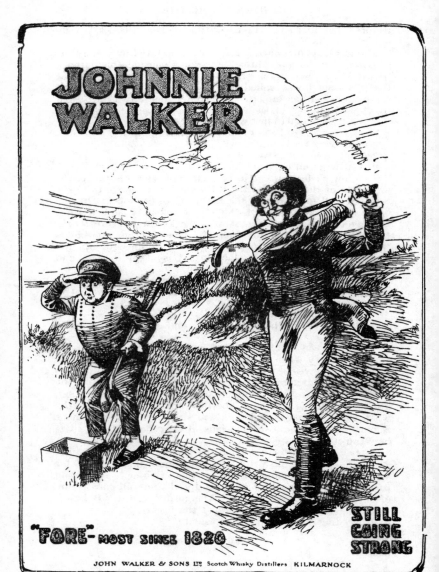

" An' you ma' lad. Your name ? "

" Ebenezer Zaccarrini, sir."

Scratching his head and looking puzzled he said :

" Run you awa' hame laddie, you wisna' wi' them."

It was almost a daily occurrence to have a house window broken by a misplaced shot or ricochet of a ball or other hard substance and the annoyed householder was obliged to report the accident to the police. One of the many duties of the " Bobbie " was to make enquiries and try find the culprit, but firstly, details of the breakage had to be investigated and noted.

" Aye ! Aye ! Mistress, the laddies at it again. Let's see ! Aye ! Aye ! broken frae the outside."

" Noo' let's gae inside. Aye ! Aye ! Yes ! Yes ! there's the stane that did it on ye're ' bunker.' "

" Jist that. Windy broken on baith sides."

Complaints were received at headquarters of the regular " harrying " of a hen run and the " Bobbie " was detailed off to make enquiry. Hot on the trail he learned of a " tom " cat belonging to a widow, that had foraging propensities and presenting himself importantly he asked the widow :

" Uh ! Huh ! Ye're cat's in trouble : Fat's its name ? "

Reply : " Jock."

" He or a she ? "

" Is ye're cat in ? "—whether the cat was to be subjected to cross examination or such like is not known, but the widow answering the question in the negative was further interrogated :

" Whan dae ye expect him ? "

In many of the tenement houses a practice is common for the tenants to have " their day " of the communal wash-house situated beside a row of coal cellars in the back yard.

An earnest housewife brought her old-fashioned round tub with its contents to the wash-house.

These tubs were usually made from an old barrel, two of the staves, one on either side, being left longer and pierced to form the handles. After arriving at the wash-house and depositing her " washing " she remembered that her " pot of broth " was on the fire and hastened back to temper the heat. In her absence—a neighbour as a practical joke, put the tub and contents in an adjacent coal cellar. Back came the washer-woman to find her tub gone and fearing the worst, reported the " theft " to the " Bobbie." After getting

B

details of the "theft" the "Bobbie" asked "Whit kind o'
a tub wis it ? "

"A roond tub, Geordie, with handles on each side."

"Oo'! Aye! a round tub with handles."

"Wid ye ken ye're ain tub again, mistress ? "

"Brawly, Geordie, ain o' the handles wis broken."

"Aye! Aye! that's evidence. Wis it the left han' or
the richt han' handle that wis broken ? "

Tarry Dan

A worthy at the Docks 40–60 years ago. He owned an
old fishing coble to which he frequently gave a fresh coat
of tar, and gave rise to the report that the application was
necessary to keep it from falling apart.

He earned a meagre living from taking parties a sail round
the tidal harbour, but seldom or ever, went outside the pier
head. His reason for not venturing "out" was probably
the extra physical exertion required in the heavy tide-way
and risking his young cargo to the elements. The tariff
was 1d. per round of 15 minutes, collected before weighing
anchor.

At "tide time" when the dockgates at the entrances
to "Earl Grey" and "King William" docks were open
was Tarry Dan's harvest and many thousands of pedestrians
must have blest Dan for ferrying them across the open
lockway when they were in a hurry to catch the pleasure
steamers, or going to the baths. There were no swing bridges
then and the pedestrian who failed to see the warning flag
on the Pilot and Dockgate house had to "shanks naggie"
it back round the Customs House or through the Royal Arch.

The Worthies O' Dundee
by F. W. S.

I will do what I can, I am a Dundee man,
  If you listen unto me ;
I hope you will tell if I do gae wrang
  About the Worthies o' Dundee.

There was a little man called Waterloo
  That carried a muckle stick,
And if you cried out Paddy's craw
  You was sure to get a lick.

Peter Powrie and Jelly Feet,
  And Sneeky Moo and his brot,
And Trokie Knows, and Docherty,
  His face as clean's the pot.

There was Sandy Young and Fraser,
  And worthy Davie Rait,
Chaw Nails and Charlie Gray,
  Coffin Shepherd and his crape.

There was Humphy Kate and Fechtin' Nell,
  And drunken Andrew Buddie,
Brimstane Bet and Skipper Bell,
  And Saut and Whitening's cuddie.

Tattie Jean and Fiddler Tam,
  And sporting Fanny Brown,
Policeman Scobbie and Mr. Taws
  Then the hale force o' this town.

Daft Nosey Jack and Hairy Kale,
  The bellman o' the Hill.
Blind Andrew Drummond, that often sang
  The Lass o' Pattie's Mill.

Daft Magdalene and Fire Nannie,
  And daft Jean Tyrie, too,
And Humphy Jonnie wi' his blue,
  And the showman Mealy Poo.

Dazy Ingram and Dozzy Lamb,
  And Rusty Needles and Preens,
Flukes and Treacle, the Dirty man,
  Mrs. Stalker and her greens.

And ane amang the council
  Was little Willie Blair,
The Laird o' Tipperary,
  For an M.P. he tried sair.

Blind Hughie, too, we canna pass,
  For he had songs in store ;
You can mind the bellman wi' the ass
  And Razor at the shore.

Little Jamie, wi' his lum hat,
  That gaed and begged his bread,
Mr. Campbell the session clerk,
  Geordie Mill that stole the dead.

Mr. Fuz the showman,
  Betty Blair that selled the tripe,
Birdie Hynd the cobbler,
  Mrs. Lyall the big fish wife.

Johnny Dye the chimney sweep,
  Stormont the auctioneer,
Mick Leaburn in the market,
  And Baker the big leer.

Joe Dempster the bellman,
  Cried the empty bag wi' the cheese,
Johnny Wood, the merchant,
  That deals amang the greese.

Fat Keiller and Saut Cowan,
  Twa cautions, market chaps,
Charlie Harris the bellman,
  Mrs. Grant among her slops.

Take-an-egg Mearns,
  And little Piloty Tosh,
Tarry Jack and Cowheel,
  The cooper Tammy Ross.

Farfar Tam the writer
  As smart a chap ye'll see,
Has got himsel' weel feathered
  Since he came to Dundee.

Peter Neucater and his scutcher,
  And Captain Johnny Lee,
The oldest skipper in the trade
  Between Kingoodie and Dundee.

Tam Wighton and cripple Crichton,
  Dilse Charlie and his barrow,
Candy Kate and Tuffy Reid,
  The carter Willie Harrie.

London spices Geordie Sweeny,
  The Russian Geordie Crow,
And sweetie Tammy Tennant,
  That lived in Thorter Row.

Little Jockey Alexander,
  And Brand that selled the saut,
Tripe Shearer into Fish street,
  And a pub called John o' Groat.

Parochial Johnny Cogan,
  And a beagle some called Ross,
If you did not pay your rates
  They showed you they were boss.

Mr. Leng, the king o' papers,
  And praying Davie Begg.
Scabbie Joe and Langshanks
  The ghost o' Chapelshade.

Captain Davie Edwards
  O' the Star o' Tay,
Jock Elphiston the scraper,
  And little Jockey May.

Big John Bog the Beagle,
  To roup you he wasna shy,
Charlie Walker the cadger,
  The jailer cutter Mackie.

James McFu the lawyer,
  And sporting Flowerdew,
Lang Tam Abbot the beagle,
  And detective Jamie Dow.

Hill, the lovely tenant,
  Mackie upon his horse,
Mr. Parr and Mr. Lamb,
  Our consequential force.

King Coffee and Heather Heels,
  Among the common tribe,
Beveridge and Naiggie,
  Their high horse full doth ride.

Among the harbour porters
  There was lang Sandy Brown,
Honest Trokie and John Dorward,
  A credit to the town.

Brownlee, ex-Provost,
  That put himsel' in a state,
Gave Peter Graham the hundred pounds
  For stealing the silver plate.

Mr. Bisset the beagle,
  A cauld ill-hearted loon,
And canny Mungo Ritchie,
  Big Steel that kept the Crown.

Jocket Stewart the runner,
  Sandy Fields the crimp.
Bobbie Waddle the tailor,
  A cheeky little imp.

Poor Mag Gow, the cadger,
  And the female Jack Mackay,
M'Gonagal the poet,
  Kitty Luckie wi' her kye.

Funny Tammy Fraser,
  Little fat cabby Gray,
Drunken Wullie Christopher,
  The showman Mr. Day.

P. O'Neil, professor,
  Robbie Salmond wi' his bread,
Sold sweeties, gingerbread, a' in lots.
  At sixpence overhead.

Black Mag and Tammy Tamson,
  Pie Snaps into the Hill,
And muckle Nosey Anderson,
  That wrought in Dease's Mill.

Mr. Arthur the scavenger,
  And sanitary Tam Kinnear,
That made his wife so odious,
  To divorce her he tried sair.

Mr. Tammas Powrie,
  The showman Jamie King,
And canny Sea Pie Davie,
  And the sailor Tam M'Queen.

Honey Tam the cadger,
  Stout Cooper and Stout Scott,
Cripple Willie and Piper Cameron,
  Tumley Down the drunken sot.

Collins the comedian,
  And Mr. D. B. Brown,
And Rennie the policeman,
  That kept the cheepers down.

Mr. George O'Farrel,
  A man that kept a pop,
And muckle Bubbly Tammy,
  And Livingstone the fop.

The great Gilroy, a spinner,
  The Provost wi' his ale,
He was a man of consequence
  And no like Neely Steel.

The ane sold ale in pitchers,
  The other an ounce of tea,
Neely sold to auld wives,
  He the ragtag o' Dundee.

And sturdy Bailie Gentle,
  A man wi' lots o' sense,
He liked aye to hae a shine,
  But at the town's expense.

Jock Rattray and his auld horse,
  The carter Muzzel Joe,
And Simon wi' his bagpipes,
  He prided them to blow.

And cheeky Mr. Piper Gray,
  But we manna him despise,
Daft Baubie, Mae Luck that way,
  And Athole wi' his pies.

Jock Maxwell and his apples,
  Fish cadger Andrew Dand,
Bobbie Clement, and Tailor Third,
  A cheeky little man.

Teetotal Jamie Scrimgeour,
  Did Temperance Lectures thump,
At meetings, concerts, and soirees,
  He aye was there to stump.

But of a' the lots I mentioned here
  Of Worthies great and sma',
Pie Jock been up and in the moon
  Wi' Jock o' Aranha.

Twa Jocks they had a gill or twa,
  Frae a man into the air,
Then they entered in the moon,
  To see a' what was there.

There was lots o' thieves and hangmen,
  Reading the Weekly News,
And lots o' lean' policemen,
  Mrs. Collins and skipper Blues.

There were ministers and lawyers,
  And doctors there also
And lots o' them that couldna' live
  At peace wi' us below.

The same twa worthies had a booze,
  Pie Jock he wanted hame,
And through the clouds cam' tumblin' down
  And landed in Trades Lane.

So noo my ditty's ended
  I hope there's nae offence
And if you like to mend it,
  It is at your ain expense.

Fizzy Gow's Tea Party

Kind freen's I'm here again, I've just come out afore ye,
To sing anither sang, cause ye kindly did encore me,
  I like to see ye a' my freens, say smiling gay and hearty,
  The sang I'm gaun to sing to you, is " Fizzy Gow's Tea
    Pairty."
Chorus : Lall a dall a dae Lall a dall a dae
        What fall a daddy fall a dall a dae.

Now the pairty it was held, in the holy land o' Fish Street,
Fish heads and tatties, Athol pies and pig's feet,
  Fire's Nanny she came in, swore she wad cook " Cow Heels "
    goose,
  And " Hairy Kale " cam running in, he'd hooked it frae
    the Poorshoose.

Now they called on " Hughie," for a song,
To keep the pairty running long,
  When " Mag Gow " she got up a knife, an' swore she'd
    stab Auld " Andra Buddy,"
  She missed her mark, the knife run in the tail o' Fizzy's
    Cuddy.

Now " Fizzy " swore by the death o' his auld cuddy,
And for the " Razor " tae the dock they sent off Andra
    Buddy,
  And when the " Razor " he came in, Waterloo he was'na
    hearty,
  And him and Mag got sixty days o'er " Fizzy Gow's Tea
    Pairty."

Worthies of Dundee

It's noo, my lads, I'll sing a sang,
  An' sure I am it's new,
Altho' the characters I'll name
  Hae lang been kent by you,
There's first Pie Jock, syne Jelly Heel,
  Then Hairy Kail at shore,
Wi' Chaw Nails too, an' Charlie Gray,
  Twa lads that drink galore.

Chorus : Yet fam'd tho' these may be in toon,
  Pie Jock still dings them a' ;
For he's been up an' roun' the moon,
  Like John o' Arran Ha'.

Noo see the Jolly Beggar, low
  Wi' snack mou' in his throat,
Wi' Troaky Nose an' Docherty,
  His face as clean 's the pot ;
Then Davie Rait an' Sandy Young,
  An' Frazer, oor gude drummer,
Wi' Pie Snap too, an' Fussie Gow,
  An' Fire, the ill-tungued limmer.
      Yet fam'd tho' these may be in toon, &c.

There's Singing Hughie, he comes next,
  'Mang singers he's a king,
Then Cadger Jamie Williamsom,
  Wi' haddocks, cod, or ling ;
Syne Bob Watt, bawlin' dilse an' tangle,
  Wi' Coffin Blake perch'd on his box,
Deck'd in cravat an' crape.
      Yet fam'd tho' these may be in toon, &c.

Then Piper Simson comes by chance,
  An' up his bag he blaws,
Till Tailor Third gets up tae dance,
  But's seized by Gashie Taws.
Next in the fray comes Jamie May,
  Wi' funny Andrew Buddie ;
An' by the by, the sweep-lum Dye,
  Wi' Saut an' Whitin's cuddie.
      Yet fam'd tho' these may be in toon, &c.

Nae doot this sang is somewhat lang,
  But yet before I close,

B*

J. B. HAY & Co.,
Builders and Contractors.

Synthetic Stone
A
Speciality.

☐ ☐

Building
Demolition
and Repairs.

Lancashire Boiler Seats Built In.   -:-   *Ferro-Concrete Work.*

JOBBING CAREFULLY ATTENDED TO.

Office and Yard—   'PHONE 2507.

61 SOUTH TAY STREET.

R. M. LINDSAY & C⁰.

Electrical Engineers

High-class Electrical Installations
by Modern Methods

•

POWER, LIGHTING, HEATING
WIRELESS, ALL APPLIANCES

Stores : Wellgate, Dundee

TELEPHONE 3356

74 MURRAYGATE ∴ DUNDEE

I hae twa ither characters
  O' which I maun dispose—
Then Stormouth comes, the Auctioneer,
  O'Farrel comes an' a'
An' if Auld Horny wants a leear,
  Dundee can furnish twa.
        Yet fam'd tho' these may be in toon, &c.

The Worthies of Dundee

Ae nicht feeling drowsy, I had a bit stroll,
As far as the Provie wi' auld Wullie Croll.
We went intae the Stag on oor road comin' back,
Jist to hear a bit sang, or a wee social crack.
Big Peter the Tinkie was there playin' jigs,
Fidgy Mick he was waltzin' wi' twa Glesca' prigs.
But when Auld David Shinem he jined in the dance,
Poet MacGonigal hadna' the ghost o' a chance.
Honey Tam and Gouk Lowden were dressed to some tune,
Likewise Fizzy Gow and the famous Muldoon.
Geordie Tasker, Dulse Charlie, and Big Candy Bob,
Were discussin' Home Rule wi' the great Sandy Robb.
Matty Big Toe the snoozer, Fly Mick and Blue Jock,
Were there wi' Match Patty and Auld Cheeky Rock.
Coo Heel, being chairman, who felt rather big,
Proposed Donal' Blue for a guid Irish Jig.
Peter screwed up his drones to the tune o' quick time,
When the jiggin' and dancin' was something sublime.
Then the Chairman cries oot " It's MacGonigal's turn,
For his noble recital o' famed Bannockburn."
Blind Hughie rose up, gave his mooth a bit traw,
He sang "Auld Robin Gray" and " My Nannie's Awa '."
And Auld David, the Fiddler, he's a man that's no' blate,
Gave them a bit stave o' " Oor Little Kate."
They got mixter-maxter and kicked up a row,
And Shinem he scattered the great Fizzy Gow.
Honey Tam and Gouk Lowden got clear o' the scrape,
But the Tinkie's physog. was knocked clean oot o' shape.
The fech o' the worthies has lang passed awa'.
They fear nae the cauld blast, the drift, nor the snaw.
On oor street, lane or market, nae mair they are seen,
So we will noo drap the curtain o'er the worthies that's
    been.

Father Shinnam

A barrel merchant in the Hilltown district who came by his cognomen in the following peculiar way :

On his rounds collecting old flour, treacle, oil or other barrels he had a horse and cart and was usually accompanied by his son. One day the horse " cast " a shoe. The son remarked " shin-im (shoe him) Father, Father shin-im, an' I'll haud his heid " and ever afterwards the cask merchant was so named. Another version is that the father was engaged in a fight with a carter and the son advised his father to " Shin 'im, father, and I'll haud the horse." (Shin 'im— to kick his opponent on the shin.)

One day a slater was repairing the roof of a two-storey tenement and thinking his exalted position was his protection shouted " Father Shinnam." Father promptly took down the slater's ladder and left him " alone in his glory."

At intervals Shinnam got a supply of barrels which had contained treacle and the young lads knocked an end in and cleared out the residue of treacle with sheets of brown paper. Woe betide the innocents these laddies met, who were rendered temporarily sightless.

Belly Go First

A hawker who lived in the " Blackie " (Blackness) quarry was of enormous Falstaffian proportions and the appellation was given after this incident.

The " Cat's Close " a very narrow passage, still extant, between the Scouringburn (Brook Street) and the Blackness Road was the scene of the following humorous incident. The boys waited until the hawker was approaching the " Cat's Close " and made remarks relative to the paunch of the hawker, and on his showing fight they ran up the close with the hawker in full chase. The boys got through the passage way, the hawker stuck.

Daft Bob

A " personality " on the streets 30 years ago.

Bob carried about with him a board on which he gave a performance of which no description would convey to the reader any idea of its merits ; it was not a dance, it was not acrobatic and no effort was made as to rhythm. None of the fantastic dances of the modern school could equal Bob's Terpsichorean efforts and as a new step came to his mind his shouts would cause envy in the heart of an Indian chief if he had been present. Bob usually finished his performance by balancing either his cap turned upside down or the dancing board on his head and endeavoured, seldom with success, to stand on one leg. Bob sometimes was cajoled to turn a " Summery " (Somersault) and very clumsily emulated the young boy who did a Cat-ma. Bob usually prefaced his tricks by shouting " Look at this fake I'm da-in," and to the ladies in his audience " Ay ye lummer," " Ay ye cuttie."

Scabbie Joe and Honey Tam

Two inseparables of the cadger class belonging to the Greenmarket. Joe was a big lanky, slouching chap with pronounced bow legs, bald and had a skin complaint which caused him much itching and hence his name. A common idea amongst the youngsters was that Joe could not catch them as all they had to do was " scud 'atween his legs " but this method was never known to have been successfully used. Tam was short of stature and fat, very dirty and wore ragged " Moleskins."

Periodically they got a stock of apples, fish, or other commodity from Mick Laburn who hired one of his two-wheeled barrows to them.

Both possessed " lungs " which were used to purpose especially when the "ragging " of the pedestrians raised their easily aroused anger. The youngsters usually irritated the pair by carolling

> " Oh ! my, I'm no cairn,
> Scabbie Joe and Honey Tam,
> Are noo' sellin' stinkin hair'in."

and when the more rowdy element upset their " apple cart " and the fruit rolled down the Hilltown and Wellgate, the cursing of Joe, the screaming of women and the howls of the youngsters could have been heard a mile away.

Honey Tam had a dislike of the police and a wag used to sing a song to the tune " Stirling Bridge " referring to one of Tam's enemies :

> On a summer aifternane
> An awfu' row began
> Between bold Charlie Pirie
> And the famous Honey Tam ;

Tam seized a knife for cuttin' cheese
And went down on his bended knees,
And swore by Lord Dundreary,
That as sure as his name was Honey Tam ;
And he lived doon in " The Holy Land,"
He'd murder Charlie Pirie.

Bung the Barrels

A contemporary of the foregoing, who used to wait at the
Dundee, Perth & London Shipping Co.'s shed the arrival of
the empty London Stout casks for transit to London. He
watched his opportunity and pulled out the cork bungs
and up-ended the cask on the top of another to catch the
lees or dregs. He and his associates then lapped up the liquor
with evident relish.

Pig's Feet

A character in the Greenmarket who possessed a voice that
could be heard from the Royal Arch to the High School,
got occasional jobs as " crier " at the shows. His engagement
on this occasion was a freak that had pig's feet where hands
and feet ought to be. His practised cry was " Come up'!
Come up : Woman with four distinct pig's feet," but after
frequent visits to Powrie's and Maggie Steel's public houses,
the word " distinct " was rendered as " stinkin' " and hence
his name.

Paddy O'Neil

A self styled " professor of physick " who carried on an
extensive business in salves and lotions in the Overgate,
60-70 years ago and who according to the words on his
gravestone was a descendant of the Kings of Ulster. He
died on the 18th December, 1880, aged 69 years, was buried
in the Balgay Cemetery and his gravestone is worthy of
inspection. It is erected on the highest part of the westmost
hill of the Balgay group and is easily distinguished by the
flaming " Red Hand of Ulster "
Then follows a genealogical tree too long to be given here.
Paddy is said to have had his coffin on exhibition in his
back shop many years before his death.

Geordie Tasker

One of the best known worthies of about 50 years ago.

A cattle drover to " profession " he was engaged regularly
in herding cattle between the railway stations at Dundee
and Lochee to the slaughter-house or to farms in the neighbourhood of Dundee.

Geordie had a " Mount Everest " between his shoulders
commonly known as a " humph."

A well-known Dundee wrestler had challenged anyone in
Dundee and boasted he could put his opponent " flat on his
back " within ten minutes." The challenge was accepted
and Geordie was introduced on the night of the contest.
One night Geordie was being treated in a well-known " Pub "
outside of which the Salvation Army was carrying on their
good work. One of the Army's vocal numbers was " Even
me, even me," when a wag suggested that Geordie should
offer himself, whilst another wag remarked " It would tak'
a steam roller to do that."

With the " immortal " poet MacGonagall, Geordie was a
frequent entertainer at the variety shows in Dundee and as
pie eater and hot porridge consumer was frequently a prize
winner. (Under the heading of Baron Zeigler, Geordie is
also referred to).

At the Submarine Miners' Annual Camp at Broughty
Ferry, Geordie was a regular visitor, particularly round about
dinner time. The mess orderlies delighted to have him there
to test his capacity. The " Kail pat " ladle was handed Geordie
to finish up a pailful of Scotch broth, before starting on a
second course of beef and potatoes—verily all going into a
seemingly " bottomless pit."

John—the Masher

John the Masher was a well-known solicitor who, after
he had lost his cash in the City of Glasgow Bank smash,
took to drink and as is usual became slovenly in his habits.

He was credited with having a developed legal knowledge
and in some phases of Law his opinion was respected. The
pseudonym—the Masher—was applied by John always wearing a tile hat as was supposed to be the proper head gear for
a writer or lawyer. John and his hat came in for frequent
rough usage, one incident being :

John was well oiled and took his stance at the side of the
potato engine that stood at Tulloch's corner (High Street—
Reform Street), attracted either by the aroma of the cooking
potatoes or the warming influence of the coke fire. Whilst

there, two ladies of easy virtue also took up their stand at the engine.

The Masher passed some remark offensive to the " ladies " when in the twinkling of an eye John's head was entirely encased in his hat and the good offices of a friendly policeman were required to restore sight to the Masher. The Masher had his usual rounds and when Bacchus had his clutches well in, John who had made himself obnoxious to " Mine Host " was thrown out and left sprawling in the " gutter." Picking himself up and appreciating his muddy condition he remarked " Well ! Well ! it gave him some trouble."

" Corkie "

A mendicant with a " game " leg who promenaded the busy thoroughfares of the town selling " Four pipes and tops, a penny," or according to his stock " twelve pipe lids, a penny." One day in the Albert Square opposite the Burns statue a blind Bible reader read out of the Book " And the Lord said unto Moses "—" Four pipes and tops, a penny " shouted " Corkie " to the immense amusement of the bystanders.

" The Iron Horse "

A young woman of Herculean strength who did a man's work in the " Tarry " work or mill at the top of Horsewater Wynd. Her mother was also named " The Iron Horse " for a similar reason.

One day in " Paddy's Market," held then at the West Port, some of the young roughs were taking liberties with the stall holders when " The Iron Horse " intervened and threatened them. " I'll pit ye on ye're backs if ye dinna stop." The roughs still persisting " The Iron Horse " carried out her threat and peace was restored.

" Dulse Charlie "

An honest, well doing worthy, who promenaded the " streets broad and narrow " with his wheelbarrow on which was dulse and tangles, calling " Dulse and tangles do you know " and when these succulent sea weeds were not procurable he sold candy of his own manufacture.

He lived in the Quarry Pend (Cowgate).

A correspondent writes : " Many a time we supplied him with a few groceries which he always paid for.

" I think I hear his voice now, " Gie's a pickle tea and
sugar and tobacco, and a bowlie o' yer potted head.
Bawbees are awfu' scarce the noo, Mistress."

A regular cry of Dulse Charlie was " a wee wheen rags
for a pickle dulse," and he was usually accompanied by a
contingent of small boys and girls, who delighted in his good-
humoured sallies to all and sundry.

Snuffy Daw

A labouring man who in 1870 was employed by a coal
merchant in Barrack Street and was addicted to snuff taking—
a very common practice of the gentry during the last century.
He lived in a rough made shed with red tiles in the Strips
of Craigie, the fire burned in the centre of the shed and the
smoke therefrom was allowed to find its own way out, whilst
his bed was a bundle of straw held in place by the side from
off a farm cart pushed into the ground.

The boys believed he lived in a cave in the Strips of Craigie
and were not keen on investigating the truth of this.   His
gaunt, forbidding appearance kept him from being molested.

Coal Mary

A small, scantily clad body who carried a bag, which she
endeavoured to fill with the pieces of coal which fell from the
carts at the disloading of the small coal vessels in Earl Grey
dock.   Whether she traded for profit or not was never known.
She was the butt for the banter of the gamins of the time,
and her retorts, as befitting one of her line of business were
of an extremely sulphurous nature.

Warts

Sixty or seventy years ago an epidemic of these skin
troubles broke out and this " quack " made a good living
in the following peculiar manner.

His stock-in-trade was a large sheaf of straw and the
afflicted paid him 1d. per wart for his " cure " which was a
joint from the stem for each wart.

The patient had to carry these joints of straw in his hand
and find out where a funeral was taking place, and at the
first movement of the horses, had to throw the joints under
the hearse—" and all the warts faded again."

DUNDEE BOARD OF DIRECTORS

JAMES BARTY, Esq., LL.B.
J. ERNEST COX, Esq., LL.D.
CHARLES C. DUNCAN, Esq.
JAMES FENTON, Esq.
J. A. KYD, Esq.
C. H. MARSHALL, Esq., S.S.C.

FIRE
—
Burglary
—
Marine
—
Fidelity Guarantee
—
Plate Glass
—
Third Party
—
Motor Cars

THE NORTHERN

FIRE   LIFE
ACCIDENT   BURGLARY
ESTAB? 1836

ASSURANCE COMPANY
· LIMITED ·
DUNDEE OFFICE
110 COMMERCIAL STREET

TOTAL ASSETS £23,370,000

LIFE
—
Annuities
—
Personal Accident
—
Sickness & Accident
—
Workmen's Compensation
—
Domestic Servants

DUNDEE OFFICE:
Northern Assurance Buildings
110 COMMERCIAL STREET.
Secretary—ROBERT BUTTER

*Prospectuses, Proposal Forms and necessary
particulars may be obtained on application.*

TELEPHONE NOS. 3094, 3095.   TELEGRAPHIC ADDRESS:
"NORTHERN, DUNDEE."

Doupie Small

A stone mason to trade, who over thirty years ago went on strike for a penny an hour on his wages, but failing in his quest he swore he would never work again; held to his word and lived to a ripe old age. He frequently took up a stance in North Lindsay Street and awaited the coming of the late sheriff, J. Campbell Smith, who was a stone mason in his young days, and this worthy old gentleman never failed to drop a coin in Doupie's hand on his way to the Law Court.

Tea-Pot Tam

A worthy of the Scouringburn district of over 60 years ago, who firmly believed he could imitate a tea-pot.

Poorly clad, he was nevertheless proud of his outsize Tammy Shanter with its big red " toorie " which same, this worthy imagined was a tea-pot lid. Every few yards, Tea-Pot Tam struck a pose with his right arm hooked in front to suggest the spout whilst his left hand was held in the centre of his back to act as the Tea-pot handle. This pose he kept until somebody lifted off the " lid " or knocked off the spout or handle, when off Tam would amble away and repeat the performance.

Kink Hoast

A knowing wag who played on the credulity of the working class by posing as the curer of the Kink Hoast (whooping cough) and gathered round him a large clientele. He possessed a well groomed donkey and as to whether or not he knew of the religious belief appertaining thereto it was never known. He moved from district to district taking up his stance in little frequented alleys or back yards and awaited the coming of a distracted mother with her coughing child. The mother handed the child under the donkey's belly from one side, to a waiting relative or friend at the other, and this was thought to be a certain specific for the troublesome complaint. The charge for a child in arms was 6d., but if a " toddler " 4d.

" The Laird o' Lennox "

A very thin man with white sightless eyes, red skinned, dressed in Stuart-tartan and eked out a living by blowing

on a big tin whistle. Nobody ever knew the tunes that the
" Laird " played, but always before beginning his recital
he would strike a dramatic attitude and remark :
" Who gave me this lonesome whistle ? "
" Ah ! I mind noo'. The Laird o' Lennox."

" Snuffy Bunker "

A well-known schoolmaster in Dudhope Street, who was
addicted to snuff taking and had " capacity " on which to
indulge. Woe betide any of his scholars found emulating
their elders by smoking, which was usually from a Partan
Claw used as a pipe, in which was placed, when tobacco could
not be got, surreptitiously or otherwise, brown paper or a
dried leaf known to the boys as " Shallagy."

" Sooracks "

A working man of cleanly habits who appeared in the
East end of Dundee about 50 years ago on the Tuesdays
and Fridays with a basket suspended from his neck with a
supply of water cress and sooracks.
When he had gathered an audience he gave a short lecture
on the harmful consumption of red meat and then distributed
his vegetables among the boys and girls. No payment
was asked for. " Sooracks " was an early pioneer of
Vegetarianism.

" Dossie " Lamb and Jimmie Bonner

Two characters who paraded the streets early last century.
" Dossie " was a little bow-legged man, whilst Bonner was
powerful, well built and wore a big beard which caused fear
in the minds of the young generation. Both were eventually
confined in the asylum. The Doctor of the institution was
a believer in hard work being good for mind and body and
commanded the pair to dig holes in the asylum grounds
which when large enough, he asked them to fill up again.
Jimmie objected and said : " Well, Mr. Lamb may do it if
he likes but I'm ―― if I do."
The following story is attributed to one or other of these
worthies. At any work they were engaged in necessitating
the use of a wheelbarrow the vehicle on its return journey
was turned upside down and on the " keeper " asking an
explanation for this procedure he got the following reply :
" I'm no' daft, some loonie micht pit something in it."

Jimmy the Blind Fiddler

St. Patrick's Day in Dundee forty to sixty years ago was always the occasion of fights between the Protestants and Roman Catholics and a refrain was sung as follows :

> The Green, the Green, the dirty, dirty Green,
> The Green, the Green that shall be torn ;
> The Blue, the Blue, the bonny, bonny Blue,
> The Blue that shall be worn.

These colours were transposed according to the religious beliefs of the contending factions. In a contracted, but often more hurtful, sense, similar scenes were seen in the " Blue Mountains " at the back of Micky Coyle's public house in the Hawkhill every Saturday night. After closing hours and the majority of the customers well primed, Jimmy took his stance in the alleys behind the " pub."

An Irishman would hand Jimmy a " copper " and request " St. Patrick's Day " and after playing a few bars a Protestant would ask for " Boyne water " and so on until " Music hath charms to soothe the savage breast " was a misnomer and breasts and brain were filled with fight.

Sequel—sore heads at home and in Bell Street next morning.

Indigo Blue

An itinerant seller of blue cam whose face, either by physical affliction or the colouring matter in his wares was always of an azure hue. He hurdled all over the town crying :
" I'm Inde, I'm Inde, I'm Inde-go blue."

Gashie Tawse

Old Dundonians will remember about Gashie.

He was the first " Bobbie " appointed under the present Police Acts and he paraded the Burn and district. Gashie's mouth was simply a slit. He had no teeth. The bairns far and near cried " Gashie " at him and he did not enjoy it. One day he had a clutch of a screaming youngster, and the mother came running to Gashie, beseeching him not to take the boy to Bridewell. " Oh ! Maister Tawse, dinna tak' 'im, Maister Tawse," wailed the mother. A grim smile played on Gashie's mobile features, and he replied. " Aye, aye ; it's Maister Tawse when they're grippit, but Gashie when they're awa'." The tears prevailed and the moment the youngster was away he was yelling " Gashie, Gashie, Gashie Tawse ! "

Joseph Dempster

Joseph Dempster, the town bellman of Dundee 100 years ago was a droll character.

On the conflagration of the town churches on the first Sabbath of 1841, Joseph was requested by one of the burned-out ministers to go round with the bell and announce arrangements for public worship. " I'm sure you've gotten your prayers answered this day " said Joseph. " I've often heard you wish for a wa' o' fire round your Zion, but you've gotten as please ye for ae' week, at onyrate."

On another occasion, being bantered by the Rev. Mr. Todd of St. David's Church, Joseph replied : " Ou' aye, I've heard you preachin' about Balaam's ass, but I'll wager wi' a' your Bible knowledge you couldna' tell me what Abraham's coo said when he gied it a poke wi' his staff."

" No, I could not, Joseph, and I don't think you could either, if it had to be told."

" Hut awa' man, it just cried ' boo ' like ony ither coo."

Joseph, having sprained his ankle on the High Street, the late Dr. Crighton happened to pass and was called on for his advice. The Doctor, knowing his humour and wishing to frighten him said he feared the leg would require to be taken off. " Weel, weel," replied Joseph, " in that case, I'll rin the lichter."

The Baker Boy

(From a correspondent)

A remarkable man was Jimmy Carr, known throughout Scotland as " The Montrose Baker Boy."

When Jimmie learned the baking trade, baking was a very hard life. He just stayed at it long enough to have a spot on the top of his head worn bare and his legs bent inward through carrying heavy loads of bread on his head. Just about this time (50–60 years ago) Professor Anderson, " the Wizard of the North " was at the zenith of his fame as a conjurer, and Jimmy was inspired with the idea of emulating the extraordinary feats of the professor.

He had many qualities calculated to aid him in his aspirations. He had a quick brain, great manual dexterity, a good manner and address, ready wit and plenty of assurance.

With all these qualities and assiduous practice he soon acquired a remarkable degree of deftness and efficiency.

Then the lure of the road seized him and equipped with as few articles of conjuring apparatus Jimmy sallied forth to seek his fortune.

A favourite plan of his was to work the schools. With his ready address he could usually talk over the schoolmaster to give the use of the schoolroom and the children a half holiday to see the performance.

As the charge was only a penny, he was always assured of a good audience although the receipts did not come to much. In the evening he would open in any empty barn or smithy, or the biggest room in the village hotel; anywhere, in fact, that the proprietor would give him gratis.

Jimmy was the " wee boy " who could show Tom Shaw how to produce rabbits from a hat.

He would put a " lum hat " on a spirit stove, mix up a pancake batter in a bowl, turn it into the hat, give it a stir up and hand out picnic biscuits to the children, much to their surprise and delight. To the men he would give a glass of their favourite tipple : whisky, rum, wine or brandy all out of the same bottle. And then to see him stuff his mouth with burning tow and draw forth yards of many-coloured ribbons amidst thunders of applause.

The last time I saw Jimmy was on the Market Square of Stonehaven nearly 40 years ago, dressed in long blue frock coat with high brass buttons, knee breeches, thick worsted stockings and brogued shoes ; his hair hanging in long cork-screw curls over his shoulders, the whole surmounted by a velvet smoking cap, gaily tasselled and embroidered. He was a striking figure. It was on a Saturday night and the square was thronged with the usual crowd, but Jimmy set up his simple apparatus and performed his usual tricks with as much sang-froid as if he had been in full evening dress and per-forming in the best hall in Scotland to a select audience.

At the time the " Baker Boy " was travelling with " Professor " Anderson the government held a competition in Belfast to find out conjurers of worth to go to the Soudan and endeavour to " lay to rest " many of the superstitions of the natives. The subject of this article came out first with flying colours as a manipulator, but being afflicted with a hesitancy in his speech was turned down. In his later days he slid down the scale and eked out an existence by performing on the streets with the interlinking rings, etc. His remains are buried in Errol cemetery.

An old farm servant told the compiler the following story.

The " Baker Boy " visited a farm where he began to mystify the farm labourers and at one of his tricks he asked a " loon " for a penny which being forthcoming he made several " passes " and turned it into a 2/6 piece. The " loon " got the 2/6 to prove its reality and on the conjurer asking for its return to enable him to proceed with the trick got the following disturbing reply.

" Na ! Na ! a'll keep it at its full growth."

A leaflet with the following lines used to be distributed in the locality previous to a visit of entertainment by " The Montrose Baker Boy."

> Montrose Magician speed thine onward way,
> Of thee Montrose may well feel proud this day :
> No rival hast thou in the magic art,
> To cultivate the science or the joy impart.
> Royalty acknowledged hast thy fame,
> Our nobles do thy wondrous deeds proclaim ;
> Stern Caledonia welcomes thee once more,
> Enchantment bringing to thy native shore.
>
> Baker thou art, thou wondrous boy,
> America hast welcomed thee with joy ;
> King of all wizards, charmer of the heart,
> Ever transcendent be thy magic art,
> Reign still triumphant over all comperes.
>
> Boy ! tho canst baffle men of riper years,
> Onward and onward roam from town to town,
> Yielding to none, thine unperishable renown.

W. S. Finlay

Born in Baltimore, U.S.A., on October 5th, 1860, died August, 1928. Worked in a city lodging house where he evidently had time for reflection on the topics of the day. His principal theme for speech was against the " Lemonade Brigade " and mounted on an old soap box he would declaim on the activities of " Scrimmiger " and " Neil More." He was always shabbily dressed but liked to sport a flower occasionally. Everybody and every movement that would interfere with the workingman's glass of beer came under the lash of W.S.F. He was " glib " of the tongue and gave a " Roland for an Oliver " to many absurd questions put to him at his Sunday meetings in Albert Square. As specimens of the type of questions he was asked the following is a sample :

" Willie, could you mak' a set o' false teeth for the mouth of the Tay ? "

" Could you fit a pair o' socks on the foot of the Hilltown ? "

" Wad ye pit bigger sticks on candy apples ? "

" Would you be in favour of putting a bonnet on the head of the Law ? "

" If Lady Mary's fair, what was the colour of her skirt ? " At once came the reply :

" Green-market."

One day, W.S.F. in the course of his oration pointed to the statue of Queen Victoria and referred to the unveiling as " When the Duke hauled the sark off his granny."

Poet MacGonagall

No useless trouser encircled his groin
But in bonnet and tights we found him
And he stood like a modest tobacconist sign
With his tartan curtain around him.

(The autobiographical paragraphs in this " life " are taken, by permission, from the book written by the late John Willocks).

So much has already been written of this strange worthy that the compiler has decided to abridge very considerably the many episodes in the life of the " Poet."

He was born in the Grassmarket in Edinburgh, and after serving some time as a carpet weaver in Dundee, it is reported that on the Monday of the Dundee Fair, 1877, the Goddess of Poetry visited MacGonagall in his house in Paton's Lane and called on him to " Write ! Write ! Write ! "

Obeying the instruction he penned an effusion on the well-known divine George Gilfillan.

" All hail to the Rev. George Gilfillan of Dundee,
He is the greatest preacher I ever did hear or see ;
He preaches in a plain, straightforward way,
And people flock to hear him night and day,
Because he is the greatest preacher of the present day.
The first time I heard him was in the Kinnaird Hall,
Lecturing on Garibaldi as loud as he could bawl.
He is a charitable gentleman to the poor while in distress,
And for his kindness unto them the Lord will surely bless.
My blessings on his lofty form and on his noble head ;
May all good angels guard while living, and hereafter when
     dead."

The Furnishing Centre of Dundee

G*OOD FURNITURE*
is an Investment ——

that pays constant dividends in terms of Comfort
and Beauty. In the extensive Justice Furniture
Galleries you will find one of the largest selections
in Scotland of Bedroom, Dining-room and Lounge
Furniture, varying widely in Design and Price
but all thoroughly dependable in Quality and
representing Value at its Best

*You are cordially invited to walk
round our Showrooms at any time
Open Daily, 9 to 6; Saturdays, 9 to 1.30*

Thomas Justice & Sons
LIMITED
Makers of Good Furniture since 1872
Whitehall Street ∴ Dundee

The poet without signing his name to it put this production in the letter box of the *Weekly News* in Lindsay Street and it was reproduced in their paper the following Saturday with an editorial remark " this contribution to the literature of the 19th century was evidently the work of a modest genius, who was unwarrantably hiding his light under a bushel." A description of the poet's appearance is interesting. He was not very tall and had a slouching gait suggestive of a broken down actor ; wore his hair long as becomes a poet, a large brimmed hat and a frock coat which bore evidence of being long past its youth. This coat was worn in "Summer's heat and Winter's cold " and was a cast-off of the Rev. George Gilfillan. His face was solemn and sallow and typical of the South-west of Ireland and he had a slight cast in one of his eyes. After the initial effort referred to, the poems came forth in a steady stream and believing in the old adage " If you want a thing well done, do it yourself," Mac pushed his effusions in every hand he got a chance of.

The Rev. George Gilfillan befriended Mac during his life and flattered the poet by saying : " Shakespeare never wrote anything like this."

At the funeral of George Gilfillan, one of the largest ever held in Dundee, the " poet " appeared in an almost indescribable character costume of red, whether it was the Royal Stuart tartan, or Rob Roy or a Roman toga, has never been defined ; in his hand a huge scroll and his spindle shanks encased in flesh-coloured tights. But for the solemn occasion the " poet " would certainly have fallen a prey to the non-gloved hands of the Dundee youth of the period and been ducked in the horse-trough.

About this time a coterie took the poet in hand and wrote for him " A book of Lamentations," a most humorous, if in some parts rather " unrefined " bit of work. This reached, if it did not overstep, the laws of libel with " I was born of poor, but bibulous parents " and " My male parent was undoubtedly a man of great capacity. He could carry his besetting infirmity well, it evidently having as little effect on his venerable carcase as castor oil on a graven image."

He was no classical scholar, neither was he a profound theologian, inasmuch as he never could be made to understand the difference between " meum and teum," whilst his hazy and indistinct views with regard to the eighth commandment frequently led him into unsatisfactory debates with a gentleman in a horse hair wig.

The " poet's " attention being drawn to the aspersions cast on his parents, he tackled one of the producers (Mr. John Willocks). Striking a threatening attitude, shouted— " The bones of my ancestors cry out for vengeance," and got the reply—" The bones of your ancestors wouldn't fetch 2d. per lb. at Bradford's rag and bone store."

One day Willocks was " pushing his wares " in the establishment of a wholesale chemist when the poet entered and asked the price of Epsom salts : " Threepence a pound " was the answer. " No," said the poet, " that's not dear." Willocks interpreted " Cheap, at least ' not costive.' "

In Perth the poet went to a well-known chemist and asked the favour of a " bottle," he had no money but promised to come back and pay the account.

A fortnight after the poet asked for a repeat and the chemist reminded him of his former promise. " When are you to pay the former debt," to which came the ready reply " I'm a poet, not a prophet."

On two occasions the " poet " was presented with his portrait in oil. One, a pencil sketch of him rolled up and placed in a bottle of castor oil, the other a rude profile floating in the oil left in a sardine box from which the fish had been extracted, and in the Waverley Hotel the draughtsmen of Messrs. Gourlay, Bros., & Co., who had formed themselves into " The Dundee, Lochee and Broughty Ferry Society of Poets " presented him with an " Illuminated Address." This address was concocted by the eleven draughtsmen, each of whom used his art in adding to its beauty. The compiler of this book had a hand in the production and it was conceded that the then popular " Ally Sloper's Diploma " was not to be compared with the " poet's " Address.

Some so-called friends of mine invited me to a commemoration banquet in Lochee.

Habited, as specially requested, in the garb of my annunciation, I presented myself in due time at the feast, which, to tell the truth, was to me a perfect revelation of good things. I was received with an acclamation in every way satisfactory. In due course the chairman, evidently much affected, requested me to stand up. I did so, then all the rest, chairman included, knelt around me on their knees, and broke out into a mighty shout of " Long live the Prince of poetry, the great and glorious M'Gonagall." I was mightily affected as the audience rose to their feet, and took their seats with adoration clearly written on each face. The chairman then announced that, as a fitting and solemn sequel to this sublime spectacular effect, he had a toast to propose, and he hoped that every man present would see to it that his glass was fully charged in order that it should be drunk with all the honours " in a clean coup up and nae heel taps." This was received with a roar of applause which nearly lifted the roof, and when asked if I would have a tumbler of toddy, or a glass of whisky, I emphatically replied, " No, gentlemen, I am a strict teetotaller, and if I drink anything at all it will be a bottle of lemonade." This was instantly forthcoming and set down already decanted in a huge tumbler by the obliging and courteous waiter at my back.

" Now, gentlemen," cried the chairman, swinging his own aloft, " are your glasses charged ? One foot on your chairs, please, and the other on the table. Here's to Scotland's immortal and inspired poet, the great M'Gonagall. Hip, hip, hurrah ! " In a moment their glasses were drained, in another the well-known strains of " He's a jolly good fellow " were given over and over again with such power and effect as to be heard half a mile away.

By this time I required no persuasion to sing, recite, or make speeches, which dazzled me as well as the audience with their lurid and burning eloquence. I was happy, but thirsty ; but as the supply of aerated water was evidently unlimited, and the quality all that could be desired, the dry, crackled feeling in my mouth was never allowed to continue long. Anon I began to feel an inclination to embrace every one who came near me, and on the waiter setting my last drink on the table from behind, the tears of gratitude welled from my eyes, and I turned and blessed him with a subdued pathos, which greatly affected the courteous, honest, and kindly old fellow.

I staggered to the place recently occupied by my chair, and collapsed on the floor completely " hors de combat."

When I awoke to consciousness with my cheek skinned, my knee bruised, and found my wallet with my manuscripts gone, I firmly believed I had been poisoned at the instigation of some jealous rival ; but the doctor who was called—to my utter surprise and horror—diagnosed the case as a simple drunk, and prescribed the taking of a blue pill and the pledge. I took them both, and kept the latter. About mid-day, when I was able to move, I rose and found my inspiration coat like the county of Cromarty, abounding in detached portions, at which I wept copiously, and at once proceeded in righteous wrath to Lochee.

I called on the chairman, a most respectable and respected man, who for the past fifty years had been prominent in every good work connected with the dark suburb, and entered his shop tattered and seedy as I was, I struck my best tragic attitude, and belched forth in anger and anguish, " Who steals my purse steals trash ; 'tis something, nothing, 'twas mine, 'tis his, and has been slaves to thousands ; but he who filches from me my good name robs me of that which not enricheth him, but makes me poor indeed."

" What's like the maiter wi' ye, poet ? " he questioned urbanely. " Have ye lost anything ? "

" Oh, no," I answered with all the irony and sarcasm I could muster, " Solomon says ' A good name is better than riches.' Shakespeare copies and endorses the sentiment, but I question if either of them ever dreamed of such an experience as I passed through last night. I was robbed of my means of livelihood—my precious wallet, my senses and my self-respect were stolen, my good name was filched from me, and all at one fell swoop, and you ask me if I have lost anything. I have lost everything, sir ; but like poor, blind Samson— who also was made the sport of the Philistines—I will have my revenge, and pull your temple of Dagon on the top of you all, though I myself should perish in its ruins."

To do the man justice, he exhibited no guilty feeling, but bore my black and scrutinising looks, my uplifted stick, and my fierce denunciations without flinching, and calmly assured me in unmistakable accents of sincerity and truth that he knew nothing whatever of the vile whisky-drugging plot, and imagined until lately that I was drinking undiluted lemonade every time. He also told me that it took him from 11 p.m. till half-past one next morning to convey me from the Albert Hotel, where the affair took place, to my home in Paton's Lane, and as he had to carry me all the way, his only surprise was that I was not more severely battered, as on four or five occasions I slipped over his shoulder on to the hard, frosty road, his sole reward at the end of the journey being a fearful tirade of abuse from my justly indignant spouse. But as he sympathised with me to the extent of a new coat and a few shillings, I forgave him freely, convinced he had nothing to do with the matter except acting as chairman to a pack of blackguards, and the good Samaritan to me.

I am initiated into the Order of the Bath and receive a Cheque

Oh, had he lived 'mong ancient Greeks
He wad been crooned wi' laurels ;
Instead of wearin' cast-off breeks,
And livin' on dry farls.—*Prize Poem.*

I called on the gentleman referred to in my last chapter, expecting sympathy and solatium ; but before I had time to open my mouth he called me a drunken beast, having evidently heard of the Lochee exploit. " Sir," I cried, losing my temper, " You are a liar, and that is strong language for a poet to use." " Clear out," he retorted, " and don't call here again." For three weeks I did not, and was very miserable in consequence. At the end of that time a mutual friend gladdened me with the news that Mr. So-and-So was anxious to see me in order to apologise.

I hastened to his place of business at the shore, and, approaching him with a half bashful confidence, said, " I understand, sir, you are prepared to apologise for calling me a drunken beast."

" I am, poet," he frankly rejoined. " When I called you by that dreadful name, believe me I meant the opposite of the reverse."

" Thank you, sir," I replied, " I can see now that it was only the want of ignorance on your part, and I am fully satisfied with your apology," and tendering my hand with a smile, something entered the palm of it with the feeling of a red hot needle. On looking I saw it was a copper tack, and foaming with righteous rage, I at once rushed at him with my stick uplifted, when he cried vehemently, " Hold, poet, hold. I am woefully disappointed in you. I was reading this morning that General Grant, and, in fact, all great Generals, were always coolest on the point of attack, and resolved first opportunity to see if great poets were the same. Unfortunately, I see they are not, and I am more sorry than you can imagine."

Calming at once, and seeing the point, I told my friend —whom I was very anxious to conciliate—that he should have given me due warning, and I would have stood it like a martyr ; then stretching forth my hand with the mien of a spartan under torture, I said " Try it again, please, and I'll not flinch a single inch." But here the incident closed without further experiment, and that tack after all, instead

A "WORTHIE" WHISKY
SINCE
1831

STEWART'S

CREAM OF THE BARLEY

SCOTCH
WHISKY

Blended and Bottled in
DUNDEE,   SCOTLAND

of causing more bloodshed, only rivetted our friendship closer.

I am a playwright as well as a poet. My *magum opus* in this direction is a manuscript which took me six months to compose, and nearly half that time to write out. It is a tragedy of the Shakespearean type, and is entitled " Jack o' the Cudgel," in seven acts. I tried to keep it in the legitimate bounds of five acts, but became so intensely absorbed in my subject that the end of act five was reached with barely half of my characters killed.

In this dilemma what was I to do ? Two modes of procedure presented themselves. I could rewrite it in a condensed form, which would enable me to dispose of my heroes and heroines with less talk and more action ; or I could let the plot run to its natural conclusion irrespective of its length, and allow the party to whom I sold it to cut it down to suit himself, or make two plays of it for that part, so long as I got my money for it. This course I eventually decided to adopt, entirely for the reason that, so well pleased was I with its contents and general arrangement, that I could not bring myself to alter a single syllable.

It is simply perfect in phraseology, balance, design, plot and general excellence, so I finished it, and carefully put it past as a source of income if I happened to fall on evil times. It is, in fact, my reserve fund. So long as I stuck to the loom no serious evil times came ; they waited till I began to write poetry, which would not sell. The genius impelled me to write, but she had evidently no control over the sales department ; and so on one occasion, when the larder had been empty longer than usual, I took my manuscript of " Jock o' the Cudgel " to Mr. Hodges, the genial manager of Her Majesty's Theatre in Dundee, to get it valued. He advised me, if I wished to sell it, not to part with it for less than £100. I thanked him, and departed to seek a merchant.

Someone, I forget whom, told me that a good actor, a fellow-countryman of my own, Gardner Coyne by name, was that week appearing at Johnnie Wood's theatre in the Seagate, and that he thought, as Gardner had plenty of coin, and was raising a company of his own, he would be a likely buyer. To Johnnie's theatre, therefore, my manuscript like a little family Bible under my arm, I accordingly hied, and found my prospective customer and his wife the sole occupants of the little brick building. After introducing myself with my best stage bow, salaaming three times to

C

the lady, I tapped the tragedy under my arm with the fore-finger of my right, and asked if he was in the market for a play as good as any of Shakespeare's. He smiled a little, and asked me to leave it with him till next day, and he would give me an offer for it if it suited. It was a fearful risk, and I did not sleep that night, for I had left it with him without any security. On presenting myself next day, he said " I have looked through your tragedy, and am prepared to give you half a crown for it." At first I thought he meant to pay me that sum for the look he had had at it ; but as soon as he made it apparent to my astonished ears and senses that he meant his thirty dirty coppers to be the purchase price of it right off, I faced him like a lion, and wrenching my precious document from his hands, shouted in the hearing of his wife and one or two smiling " toffs," " Sir, if that tragedy was boiled in muck you would not get a spoonful of the broth for half a crown."

The Order of the Bath

This " order " was conferred in the premises of the Young Men's Club at the Nethergate end of Tay Street, who " left the poet in the bath with his silk hat and poems around him."

My best business was done generally amongst grocers, who often, in addition to the legitimate price of the poetry, would hand me a piece of well-matured cheese or a blown tin of beef to carry home with me.

Well do I remember the first time the demon of discord was let loose. It was in a grocer's shop in the Hawkhill during the absence of the " boss " through illness. I was politely asked into the back shop for the purpose of exhibiting my latest production. No sooner had I unslung my wallet and laid some dozen or so of them for inspection on a soap box, than the air was literally darkened with volleys of split oranges, rotten apples, and putrid eggs, which burst on my devoted head with the force and precision of hand grenades. My natural impulse was to attack, stick in hand, but my first rush at the foe was the last ; my improvised counter, the soap box gave way in front of me, I falling prostrate over it, hurting myself severely with protruding nails. From this unromantic position I was rudely revived by a torrent of water from a hose, which played impartially all over me. In my blind retreat to evade this I backed into the open hatchway, and fell into the cellar, which, fortunately for me, was not many feet from the shop floor, and plentifully furnished with straw. On this I lay dazed for a few moments, then gathered myself together, and proceeded in haste to the police office, where I was coolly informed by the Lieutenant on duty that " they really could not be annoyed any more with me and my complaints."

Fortune at this time favoured me by an introduction to Baron Zeigler, who ran a variety entertainment at the old circus at the back of the Queen's Hotel. I told him of my quandary without reserve. He sympathised, and offered me a week's engagement as a trial at a reasonable figure. It did, indeed, prove a trial to both of us. The first night I appeared there certainly was a little undue excitement amongst the audience, and some throwing of objectionable and dangerous missiles ; but on the whole I was allowed to proceed in comparative peace with my famous " Bannockburn," which was applauded to the echo. Next night, however— shall I ever forget it ? Never ! I shall carry its memory as well as its marks to the grave. Until that night I never for a moment imagined that there were so many veritable fiends in all Europe, let alone Dundee. To understand the proceeding thoroughly, it is necessary to give you a slight idea of the geographical bearings and general construction of the building.

Being formerly used as a circus, it is almost unnecessary to premise that the interior was round. The stage projected into the ring from the east end of the shape of a three-quarter circle, round which, some four feet below, the orchestra was seated. Directly in front, and facing the stage, with their backs to the west, sat the sixpenny ticket-holders. On the north were the fourpenny seats, packed like herrings in a barrel from floor to ceiling ; and on the south, directly across the platform, were the two and three shilling chairs, more or less comfortably filled. Between the fourpenny and the two shilling seats ran the shilling promenade, the floor of which was the roof of the entrance to the stage for the performers. It was from this elevated " coign of vantage " that the unrehearsed proceedings started.

As soon as I emerged from under it, and had just reached the platform, arrayed in my Celtic garb, with sword and buckler complete, strutting as proud as a peacock, a whole big jute bag full of soot was emptied right over me. I would have turned and fled, but the little Baron was behind me shoving me forward with his stick, and shouting " Don't be a coward,

The House for Drugs —

Davidson & Gray, Ltd.

Directors : JOHN GRAY, T. R. BROWN

Chemists & Wholesale Druggists

128a Nethergate, DUNDEE

Wholesale Business Hours :

8-30 a.m. to 6-30 p.m.   WEDNESDAY to 1 p.m.

Telephone : No. 2133.   :   *Telegrams :* " Gray, Chemist, Dundee."

Telephone No. 7464

Office :   *Garage :*

224 KING STREET   **BATH STREET**

BROUGHTY FERRY

Tyres and Accessories   Petrols - Oils - Greases

Garage Accommodation
:: for Private Cars ::

DAY AND NIGHT SERVICE

WATT'S MOTOR GARAGE

Motor Hirers, Engineers and Agents

BROUGHTY FERRY

M'Gonagall. Let the devils see there's pluck in you yet. If you show the white feather now, by G— they'll wreck the bloomin' place in 'arf a mo.'' Thus urged, I walked boldly forward to the far end of the stage, and had only time to say in tones of mortal anguish, '' Gentlemen,'' when an unparalleled atrocity occurred. Boots, beef tins, rotten eggs, and bricks showered around me, and with such force were they hurled that such of them as missed me ricochetted from the platform right into the plush chairs beyond ; one navvy's boot catching a white-haired old gentleman right in the jaw, and flooring him completely. From this place a general stampede took place, the orchestra finding safety for themselves and their instruments below the scene of action. They were lucky, for the mad rush of the chair-holders over the sixpenny seats between them and the door led to a general engagement, and many went down in that awful mêlée.

All this time the batteries from the fourpenny side— far from being silenced—were keeping up a brisk fusilade, having, I imagine, succeeded in procuring a fresh supply of ammunition, a portion of which, in the shape of a huge brick, at length caught me right in the stomach, when, like '' Abner, dean of angels,''

> '' I smiled a sickly kind o' smile,
> And curled up on the floor,
> And the subsequent proceedings
> Interested me no more.''

The poet was at this period annoyed at the interference of the police authorities and decided to make a personal appeal to Her Majesty Queen Victoria.

I have written scores of times to Her Most Gracious Majesty the Queen, have addressed Gladstone, Wolseley, and all the other '' big bugs '' in the land, and have waited in vain for enclosured answers with a deferred hope, which has nearly driven me sane. At length I resolved to call on Her Majesty personally, all other resources here having failed. No sooner was this resolved on than it was carried into effect, and I walked on foot to the Deeside home of the Queen with anything but a *decided* success.

Leaving Dundee one glorious summer morning, I determined to go to Balmoral, and lay all my grievances at the foot of the throne in person. I resolved, after reading—as I myself modestly aver I only can—such pieces of my own to Her Majesty as seemed to me most calculated to impress her and stir up her royal emotions, to put the question plainly to her whether I had deserved the treatment I had got at the hands, feet, and lungs of her Dundee subjects. But, alas, misfortune still dogged my heels.

To give my readers some little idea of my public spirit, sense of duty, and indomitable pluck, I may mention that on starting my commissariat consisted solely of half a pound of cheese and six oatcakes ; while the exchequer amounted all told to one shilling and fourpence. Of course, I made no provision for a return journey, relying on the assumption that the royal sense of justice would perceive the utter incongruity of the compiler of so much sublimity grovelling in a single-roomed den ; while minor stars, not fit to be named in the same breath as Shakespeare and myself, revelled in sumptuous luxuriousness.

So far as " togs " were concerned, my fears centred most completely on my boots. As I surveyed them they actually gaped at me. Fancy how they yawned after sixty miles through a dreary wilderness of heath and heather, with nothing to vary the monotony but thunderstorms and water-spouts, which, first reducing my paper collar to a pulp, speedily ran down inside my garments, and obtained exit at the aforesaid cracks, the utility of which I never before comprehended.

Pic-nicers and English swells dilate on the lovely gorges you pass through on the Balmoral road. I was more con-cerned about the lovely gorges which should have entered into me.

Tired and hungry, I at length arrived at the gates of the castle, which were opened by one who asked me in a southern accent what the nature of my business was. I told him I had called to see the Queen in order to demand, what she was bound to grant to the very meanest of her subjects, Justice.

" What are you ? " he asked.

" I am a poet," I replied.

" Your demand," he said sternly, " smacks more of the Anarchist than the poet, and your looks would pass for either—the same lantern jaws, hungry looks, long hair, and light blue eyes. I don't know quite where to place you."

" This is my work, sir," I rejoined, handing him the new twopenny edition of my poems. He looked carefully over it for fully five minutes in utter silence, smiling all the while.

At length he looked squarely at me, and said, " I have you now. Have you broken loose ? "

" No," I said, understanding his allusion thoroughly, " but I have broken heads in my time on less provocation."

" Oh, ho, my bold boy ; I know *your* sort. I've been a keeper myself, and have put a straight jacket on a man three times as big as you."

" You English fool," I shouted, losing my temper, " do you take me for a lunatic."

" You admitted being a poet," he coolly retorted ; " what's the difference ? All poets are fools ; hungry and ragged poets are idiots ; and a poet who thinks that Her Majesty would accord him an interview is simply stark, staring mad."

" Was your own countryman, Tennyson, mad ? " I asked.

He winced visibly at this, then said, " No, not he ; he was long-haired and long-faced, to be sure ; but he was a rich man, and a lord to boot. Moreover, he was bound to have written better stuff than you, or he would have been neither."

" Is that your standard of a great poet, ' rich, and a lord ' ? " I exclaimed in disgust. " Look here, sir, than those poems you hold in your hand (and for which you have not paid me) there is no better poetry anywhere, not even your vaunted Lord Tennyson's. He is rich and I am poor, as a man ; he is poor and I am rich, as a poet."

" Let me hear one of your pieces," he said, laughing, as if I had just said something very funny.

" No, sir," I thundered, " I am no strolling mountebank, and would not recite in the open-air to the Queen herself, let alone to one who is evidently an enemy of mine."

At this the man grew quite angry, threw twopence at me, and told me to clear out, or I would be arrested.

It began to dawn on me by this time that that man might be a friend or a relation even of Tennyson's, and when he found out that I was indeed a poet he was alarmed. So I cleared out, and he shut the gate, through which, like the righteous man of old, I had not been ashamed to speak unto mine enemy.

A reception like this would have daunted any mortal of ordinary calibre, but adversity had so long followed me that I was schooled to bear rebuffs with that equanimity which distinguishes genius from the ordinary herd. Still, being hungry, penniless, and footsore, I must confess to a temptation to shake the dust from my feet in anger against the palace gates. Nay, more, I would have done so, but from the fear that the soles might have parted in the process, and compelled me to proceed on my homeward march more like a mediæval friar than a modern poet. Therefore, with a careful sigh, I turned my back on Balmoral, disgusted at my failure, and hoping, if I could only keep from coughing and sneezing, that I and the most of my garments would arrive eventually at Paton's Lane.

We got home in company, bar the paper collar, which was totally past redemption ere I reached the Spittal of Glenshee. The boots, with the aid of lemonade wires and pieces of cord, not only held out bravely, but they looked all the more picturesque, and felt all the more comfortable, for these adventitious aids, which gave them the appearance of the foot gear of a Bedouin Arab.

I GO TO LONDON

He came, he saw, but that was all,
    The thing's beyond dispute ;
The " conquering," like the ancient Gaul,
    Was on the other foot.—*Camberwell Sneerer.*

After my return from Balmoral, I felt so downcast and fatigued that I kept the house for a whole week, during which time I had fully summed up the dismal situation. Need I recapitulate : everything had failed me, and still I was unbeaten. But if ever a man prayed fervently to get away from any place, I was that man, and that place was Dundee.

The answer to that prayer, strange to say, was brought about by a silly hoax. Heaven sent it, although the devil brought it. A letter reached me exactly a week after my return to the following effect :—

> Her Majesty's Theatre,
> Dundee, ———.
>
> DEAR MR. M'GONAGALL,—Being in Dundee, and on the outlook for a gentleman to play leading tragedy parts in London and the provinces, I would be pleased to have an interview with you, at twelve noon, at Stratton's, Reform Street, where you, I, and a few friends can have lunch together, and a talk over matters, which I hope will lead to business to our mutual advantage.
>
> Yours truly,
> DION BOUCICAULT.

Punctually at the time mentioned I put in an appearance, and was shown upstairs to a smoking-room, in which were seated ten or a dozen gentlemen, most of whom were known to me. At the head of the table was a good-looking, elderly gentleman, who was a perfect stranger. He was introduced to me as Dion Boucicault, and he looked the part so well that I thoroughly believed I had the honour of grasping in friendship the hand of the great playwright. He said he liked my appearance and the tones of my voice ; would I object to give him a specimen of my powers.

" Certainly not, Mr. Boucicault, I will only be too glad," I replied, " and if you can give me an engagement in London it will take me out of the greatest difficulty I was ever in in my life. Do you know, sir, if the magistrates of Dundee knew I was to have been here they certainly would have taken steps to prevent this meeting."

" Incredible," cried the great man in astonishment. " Envy, I suppose ; never mind. If I mistake not, the tables will soon be turned when you appear as leader of my company at Her Majesty's Theatre here, and receive a cake and wine banquet from these same magistrates. But, now to business ; let us hear you, Mr. M'Gonagall."

Thus encouraged, I gave him my own " Bannockburn," and selections from Shakespeare, Macbeth, Hamlet, and Richard the Third, until the panes in the glass roof rattled with the vigour of my declamation and the thunder of applause which followed. Boucicault was more than satisfied, and offered me £123 10s. a week, bed, board, and washing, which I at once accepted.

But now an eye-opener occurred. The lunch was called in, and judge my surprise when I found it to consist of a small glass of beer and the thinnest cut ham sandwich I ever saw or thought possible to make. I have been told that a sovereign can be beaten out to cover the front of a whole block of four storey buildings ; but the man who cut that ham, which lay between two emaciated slices of bread, could easily have covered an acre with one of Johnnie Wood's 16-pounders.

No wonder my suspicions were aroused, even although they had not left the room, laughing like to split, and tumbling over each other as they ran down the steep wooden stair, and left me all alone with the precious lunch. After thinking the matter over, I made for the theatre, saw Mr. Hodges, and had my suspicions thoroughly confirmed. Mr. Boucicault had not been in Dundee for a very long time, and the letter,

C*

which I left with Mr. Hodges, was not in his handwriting.

Mr. Hodges, it seems, had forwarded the letter to the great Dion, and he, like the large-hearted man he really was, sent me £5 by way of solatium, as he expressed it, to heal my wounded feelings. Need any one who knows me guess the brilliant thoughts which now assailed me. The finger of Providence was surely here this time. London ! Five pounds ! ! Dion Boucicault ! ! ! To London I resolved to go, and wrote to my patron Dion that I would call on him personally and thank him for his kind encouragement to a poor but meritorious poet and player, that he need not be at the trouble to meet me at Wapping, as I could call at his theatre and give him a few specimens, and that I would be greatly astonished, if he was not, concluding a remarkable epistle with a sample of native poetical genius to the effect that when the Governor among the nations at the great day examined every man's record, that

> " With thy soul He will find no fault,
> My own dear Dion Boucicault."

This, I imagined, would fetch him ; but we shall see.

With the aid of a few friends I got up a farewell entertainment, which came off quite unknown to the authorities in the Argyle Hall, which was crowded in every part. On this occasion I was presented with a ham, in the centre of which was inserted a big brass plate bearing the legend, " A meat offering from Dundee to M'Gonagall." Considering the state of the larder at the time, this was indeed a meet as well as a meat offering. On this occasion also a prize, consisting of a quarter stone of sausages, was offered for the best poem on " M'Gonagall."

This had been advertised for a week previous, and was decided at the meeting. The result was a tie betwixt two, which I give in full. As both authors felt offended at not getting an undivided award, the prize was handed to me, and though I would not take it upon me to assert that the poems were unapproachable, I do emphatically aver that the prize was, and had to be, tackled strategically. Here they are :—

> M'Gonagall, the silvery,
> Before you leave these walls,
> Before you go to London town
> To join your tragic pals.

We feel constrained to tell you,
  Before this raging crowd,
That you're a bard, and no mistake,
  Of whom Dundee is proud.

And if for two or three bob you act,
  So marvellously here ;
How will you soar in Drury Lane,
  With thousands every year.

Fare thee well, thou gifted bard,
  May fortune cheer thee ever,
And send at least, when famished hard,
  A modicum of liver.

But if neglected thou should'st roam,
  No bed, however hard ;
Take this farewell advice, and seek
  The nearest casual ward.

And write a letter to Dundee,
  Though you a penny lack,
And willing friends around you here
  Will pay your passage back.

And when you reach Victoria Dock,
  Let this dispel your gloom,
Though hard up here, you're better far
  Than in a London tomb.

The other one is longer, and also fairly good for an amateur, and runs thus :—

Robert Burns, in dulcet strains,
  Sweetly sang o' love and lasses ;
Dundee's poet, with greater brains,
  Far the Ayrshire bard surpasses.

" Scots wha hae " is very good,
  An', dootless, answered weel its turn;
But viewed as patriotic food,
  Could ne'er compare with " Bannockburn."

To "A' the airts the wind can blaw "
  We willingly wad boo the knee ;
But, Lord, it's no a sang ava
  Like " Broon haired lassie o' Dundee."

Byron's rhymes nae better fared
  Than his o' bonnie Doon ;
An' a' his English friends despaired
  When they saw thy " Silvery Moon."

England's bard, the gentle Will,
  England thocht wad still hold sway ;
Doon he drapt like half o' gill
  At the sough o' " Silvery Tay."

Ower a' the bards together put,
  Frae Friockheim to Japan,
He towers aloft, beyond dispute,
  Creation's greatest man.

Oh, had he lived 'mang ancient Greeks,
  He wad been crooned wi' laurels ;
Instead o' wearin' cast-off breeks,
  An' livin' on dry farls.

For shame, Dundee ! when he's a spook,
  His pearls may amend you ;
They re-cast here now, what says the book ?
  " They turn again and rend you."

Bouch, because a brig he planned ;
  Oh, how I blush to write it,
Was made before the Queen to stand,
  And wi' a sword be knighted.

Oh, greater Bouch, by far than he,
  Greater far, though slighted ;
A greater far than even she,
  Dubbed you, alas ! be-nighted.

This entertainment, bar the animal and vegetable curiosities
which were showered on me, proved a tolerable success, for,
besides the ham, which was well matured, as all Mr. Wood's
generally were, I got twenty shillings, part of which I had
to invest in astringents for self and all who partook of the
lively present.   Another interesting item on the programme
on this occasion was a plebiscite taken to decide whether
Shakespeare or myself were likely to be the more popular
in London, the flattering result being a dead tie, the chairman
refusing on the score of the exceeding gravity of the question
to give a casting vote, further than to say that, in his opinion,
Shakespeare and M'Gonagall were much alike, especially
Shakespeare.

For this sensible utterance I now take the opportunity of publicly thanking the gentleman, and also informing him that he did well in leaning a little in favour of Shakespeare, whom I consider about the ablest and wisest man that ever lived. I do not deny that, had I lived before him, he might have been even greater than he was, even as I am now greater, because he lived before me. Be that as it may, however, I was glad to have it in my power to tell Dion on my arrival in London of the very near squeak our mutual friend, William, had had for it.

In due time the fateful day arrived, and I presented myself at the London boat about an hour and a half before the advertised time of its departure, my only luggage consisting of a few paper collars and a supply of visiting cards, printed by a friend in Dundee on large envelopes, with the flaps cut off, something like this :—

	WM. MACGONAGALL, *L.I.A.R.*,
*Signifies	SUCCESSOR TO
Lyric Inditer	WM. SHAKESPEARE.
and	POETRY PROMPTLY EXECUTED.
Reciter.	

After waving a thousand adieus to my native land, my congregated friends, and pinching poverty, the gallant vessel steamed off, and the bard " was alone on the unconscious sea," alone to meditate on coming greatness and grandeur, now that he had immediate prospects of a helping hand from a living and successful playwriter. Having nothing to disturb the calm serenity of my soul, not even the gnawings of hunger, I gave full rein to my imagination, and allowed it ample scope to soar whithersoever it would. I saw in my mind's eye copies of my " Newport Railway " stuck all over the North Pole.

I heard the parrots in the torrid zones of the sunny south whistling in melodious accents " The bonnie broon haired lassie." I felt the sough of the plumed pines of Kamschatska as they swayed to the low and mournful cadences of my funeral pieces ; while the bird of Paradise, in heavenly hues arrayed, warbled in orange groves amid seraphic splendour my glorious " Ode to the Moon." The bul-bul, amidst the thousand glories of the primeval forest whistled in my raptured ears to the tattooed chief and his dusky squaw all the glorious symphonies of the great M'Gonagall.

T. P. FIMISTER

M.I.H.V.E.

:: *Plumber, Heating & Fireplace Engineer* ::

ARTISTIC MODERN FIREPLACES

*The most attractive and comprehensive
Showrooms in Scotland*

The variety of Fireplaces on view is probably
the largest and most varied ever displayed.

The Showroom itself, with its quiet artistic tone, enhanced
by one of the finest displays of modern etchings,
is a place of beauty and well worth a visit.

:: *A CALL IS CORDIALLY INVITED* ::

55 SOUTH TAY STREET,
DUNDEE

Telephone No. 2735   Telegrams: "Fimister, Dundee"

Branch: ST. ANDREWS
St. Andrews Telephone No. 97

I saw the " Bruce of Bannockburn " blot out as a recitation for ever the " Half a League " of my weaker English rival ; while I myself starred the London stage, with the plaudits of press and people ringing in my ears like the roar of the sea around me.

These sights and sounds soon lulled me to sleep, to be present in dreams in a more exaggerated form ; for in these dreams I imagined that the advent of the millennium was to be due mainly to the sublime literature which emanated from my fertile brain. Alternating thus between sleeping and waking visions, Wapping drew nigh, and I heard a sound of music on the shore. Thinking my patron had been at the expense of a brass band to welcome me, I asked one of the passengers, an intelligent-looking man, if he could detect the tune they were playing. My thoughts were confirmed when he stated that it was " Lo he comes to Wapping," a tune I never heard of before, but thought it most appropriate ; the only thing which puzzled me being why the composer had styled me Lochee, instead of Dundee, if I was the central idea in the flattering programme.

Wondering sore which was the true elucidation of the incident, we arrived and landed ; but no Boucicault was there, only a German band blowing away like blazes to all and sundry " Oh why left I my hame." This, my first sell in London, was both appropriate and prophetic. But as the poet somewhere remarks—

> " 'Twere long to tell, and sad to trace,
> Each step from splendour to disgrace."

From the aforesaid visions aboard ship, from the myrtle groves of Arcadia, to that beastly buggy dungeon of a common lodging-house, called the " White Horse," in Fetter Lane, surrounded by drunken blackguards, and squalor of the lowest London type ; but I suppose I must go on with it, although I am anticipating. Well, then, save the booming of some big clocks, nothing striking occurred until I reached the aforesaid " bunk," and showed the landlord my card, at which the undiscerning idiot actually laughed. Smothering my indignation with the cheering thought that the laugh would soon be on my side, I engaged a bed, for which I paid sixpence in advance, and set out for the Adelphi Theatre to see my friend.

Arrived there, I sent up my card, and the manager appeared presently, tearing it up and telling me sternly all the while that " Mr. Boucicault was too busy at any time ever to see me," and before I could either remonstrate or explain he disappeared, and, as John Bunyan would say, " I saw him no more."

This was horrible, and so dreadfully different from what I fully expected, that I actually burst into tears, and departed to seek Henry Irving at the Lyceum. Again sending up my card, another managerial looking specimen appeared " more potent than the last." After looking at me from head to foot, he asked if I really thought Mr. Irving would speak to me ?

This terrible question was asked in such scathing and contemptuous tones that I could not resist striking my most tragic attitude and belching in my deepest thunder, " Tell Henry Irving that I consider myself a far greater man than he is, and I hope we will both live long enough for him to acknowledge it."

Screwed off at the meter in this abrupt and unceremonious manner, my spirits fell below zero, and I turned my back on those two jealous actors with mixed feelings of pity and indignation, and sought the solitude of my chamber at the " White Horse." Did I say solitude ? Well, I thought I was alone till I ventured between the sheets, and then I was painfully undeceived. The only thing I was thankful for was that they were not all of one mind, as Charles Lamb puts it, or they might have pulled me on to the floor. What a restless night I did have, and yet it had its ludicrous aspect after all. One enormous fellow, shaped somewhat like a flounder, had fallen overboard into a vessel he had not calculated on, and swimming on to a raft, consisting of a spent lucifer match, he kept circling round and round in this miniature china sea, walloping his arms sailor-like, and singing lustily " A life on the ocean wave."

The situation had a serious bearing as well, inasmuch as that night's experience entirely changed my political views. Before this I was a Radical, holding, as one of the cardinal points of my political creed, that tenants should be allowed to destroy their own game. I am now a Tory in this respect, and strongly believe in the exclusive right and bounden duty of the landlord to decimate his own vermin, and leave his tenants unmolested. This explanation I heartily commend to Mr. Jenkins as quite as true, less prolix, and more practical than his mundane evolution theory. The metamorphosis can be explained in far fewer words than he uses. It was a big bug in Belfast which converted him. It was a big bug in Babylon that changed me.

After passing a miserable night I arose, cooked my own breakfast, and set out to purchase writing materials, and immediately thereafter indited two peppery epistles, one to Irving and the other to Boucicault, telling them plainly my mission in London, my expectations of assistance from them, and the disappointing result ; asking them plainly whether or not it was by their direction that their subordinates had so snubbed me, and requesting a reply in due course to the " White Horse." But no answer ever came.

I felt furious, but gradually cooled down in the exact ratio of the diminishing of my funds. Beef, you know, from its inflammatory nature, is well calculated to keep up red hot choler ; but an occasional red herring, with dry bread and terribly wet, weak tea at most irregular intervals, takes the high falutin out of a fellow wonderfully. Well then, it was after a sustained regimen of this sort that I even got so tame as to make allowances for the extraordinary conduct of those two men.

They were already at the top of the tree, I argued, and could rise no higher, even with my assistance ; while, on the other hand, the chances were that if the public saw and appreciated me, I might have gone up and forced them to come down. Be this as it may, I never got a chance, or I would not now be under the necessity of covering so much paper for a " bob."

They know it, and I know it, and it is not my fault now if the whole world does not know it. It was a strong combination, perhaps the strongest which could have been arrayed against me ; but it did not break me. At the present moment, sufficient funds provided, I am as willing as ever to try my fortune again in London.

Meantime, however, I was glad, having nothing to feed the fishes with, to commit myself once more to the briny, and leave the inhospitable hulk of a town, en route for Dundee, a poorer, a hungrier, but not a less hopeful man.

I GO TO NEW YORK

I love New York, for it made me
  Love my own land the better ;
For this I certainly will be
  Its everlasting debtor.—" *The Emigrant's Return.*"

On my return from London I was strongly urged by the

members of my own household to desert the muses, as I did not seem to be appreciated anywhere, my wife telling me that I might take it as a sign that the genius had possibly made a mistake, and brought the commission to the wrong door.

" Avaunt ! " I cried, " and tempt me not ; ye all speak about the genius as if she were a half drunk postman who mixes up his deliveries. I will never desert the post she placed me at, until she appears again and tells me to do so. Know once for all that I am irrepressible."

And I beg here and now to repeat to the whole world that, though I have been discouraged and crushed a thousand times, I have always risen again triumphant, and this is my manifesto to all whom it may concern : " I have nailed the colours of my political genius to the mast of my own appreciation, and twenty thousand demons in the shape of adverse critics cannot rend them asunder."

I say, like Martin Luther, on some of his friends trying to dissuade him from going in for a " diet of worms," ; " If every tile on every housetop was a devil, I must go on." Dundee has failed me, London has turned out a frost ; but, thank God, the world is wide, and that there are other and better places than either. I am told if I only could get to America I would soon make a fortune ; that on the streets of New York, instead of a paltry penny given grudgingly for a copy of my poems, I would get a dollar, and the buyer would feel himself the obliged party. Ah, me ! What would it be to be there ? At length a bright idea struck me, and no sooner did it do so than I put the wisely conceived plan into execution.

I got a pass book, setting forth on the first page that I wished to go to America, and that those willing to assist me in this project would have the opportunity of putting down their names as subscribers. I was successful beyond my most sanguine expectations, and felt sure that the tide had turned at last. Friend and foe alike contributed : the former I afterwards learned, to oblige me ; and the latter to get rid of what they deemed a nuisance. At the time I was blind enough not to perceive this, although my suspicions ought to have been aroused from the fact that two of the magistrates subscribed five shillings each.

It was Mr. Lamb, of Lamb's Hotel, who pointed this out to me, when I had raised sufficient money, and went to bid him good-bye. " Mr. M'Gonagall," he said, " this money

I am sure, has been given you largely by pretended friends, who want you to lose yourself in America ; but we will thwart their fell purpose yet. I gave ten shillings to help you off, but if ever you wish to come back I will send you your passage money." So saying, we shook hands and parted, I little dreaming how soon I would have to avail myself of his magnanimous offer.

Full of hope, fuller than ever, I took train to Glasgow, and was soon on board the good ship *Circassian*, in which I had secured a steerage passage.

The voyage was rough, but otherwise uneventful. On one occasion I was asked into the second cabin to give an entertainment. There was a collection taken, which I expected to receive ; but the steward intervened with the announcement that no collection could be taken on board that ship except for the lifeboat fund, and so I was done out of it, and declined all further invitations of this nature during the voyage.

On arrival at Castle Gardens, I had to declare myself a labourer. If I had said I was a poet they would have turned me back. The authorities then asked me if I had any money. I said I had, and was going to friends ; taking out all I had I asked them with as careless an air as I could assume to give me American money for eight shillings to meet immediate requirements.

I am sorry now I did not tell them the whole truth ; that I was a poet, and that all I had in the world was eight shillings. They would then have refused to allow me to proceed farther, have sent me back, and saved me a lot of misery and cruel disillusionment.

Having the address of an old acquaintance and admirer in Dundee, I took a car there, was warmly welcomed, and partook of a hearty tea, in return for which I imparted all the latest gossip from Juteopolis. Having arranged to take up my abode with my newly found friends, who were people of the better sort, we spent the evening for the most part in arranging my plan of campaign. I had with me a plentiful supply of poems and twopenny editions of my works, which I expected to clear off speedily at half a dollar and a dollar respectively. These, however, we arranged to leave alone meantime, the conclave deciding that it would be better for me to try the music halls and theatres first for a permanent engagement. Armed, therefore, with a specimen of each of my own productions, and brimful of anticipation, I started forth, not like Christopher Columbus, merely to discover

America, but more important still, to allow America to discover me.

Sauntering leisurely along in order to assimilate myself to my new surroundings, I at length reached a palatial-looking building at the corner of Broadway and some other street—which I was correct in taking for a theatre. I entered its portals, crossed the floor of the hallway, and rung an electric bell at the side of a window, on which was inscribed " Enquiry Office." In a moment the window was opened, and a gentleman in a gold laced hat and gilt buttons asked me my business.

" I want to see the manager," I said.

" Have you a card ? " he inquired.

I produced one of those I had used in London. Like all the Londoners who were privileged to receive one, he immediately commenced to laugh. I was getting sick of this, and resolved to show no more of them, the affixed initials being evidently taken too literally, and altogether misapprehended. " Friend," I said as severely as I could, " you are not laughing so much at my card as at your own ignorance. Take it to the manager at once."

With another burst of hilarity he disappeared, came back in a minute, and told me to follow him. Upstairs he went, I after him, till we reached a handsome picture-panelled door, which he opened, showed me in with a bow, withdrew, and left me standing in the most gorgeous apartment I ever saw. In the centre of this perfect room, seated at a desk, was a man about my own age, with a red face and a white moustache and goatee. Speaking with a strong nasal twang, and pointing with his finger to a chair beside me, he said : " So, so ! You air a pro-fessional liar ? Sit down."

" Sir," I said, " you have made a mistake ; I am no liar. The L.I.A.R. at my name stands for Lyric Inditer and Reciter."

" Ah ! " he said, " if I had known that I would not have troubled you. I am not interested in lyrics, good, bad, or indifferent ; and loonatics are common enough here, not to be very interesting. But I do dote on a powerful liar with a big L ; they're all the rage on this side. I perceive you air a Britisher."

" I am, sir ; and I am sorry to hear that liars are such favourites in New York."

" There's nothing else, in any line, of any use here. Are you an actor ? " he inquired.

" I am a poet and tragedian from Dundee, in Scotland,

seeking an engagement," I answered. "Of course," I continued, "if you engage me as an actor I can only speak the lines set down for me, and cannot, therefore, vouch for their veracity. But in all my poems and songs the name ' M'Gonagall ' stamped on them is a guarantee of purity and truth."

"Wall, old man, look here," he said, "I reckon you might be a tragedian without being much of a stranger to the truth, especially if you managed to steer clear of the plays of that effete old liar of yours you call Shakespeare. But if you stick no stretches in your poetry it would taste as tame as porridge without oatmeal."

In wrath, which I could only partially conceal, I pulled out my Newport Railway poem—the most moral of the batch—and, spreading it out before him, defied him to find the slightest shadow of a lie in it from Alpha to Omega.

Looking at it for two or three minutes, then holding his sides with his hands, he roared with laughter till his red face grew purple.

"Right you air," he cried, as soon as he could articulate. "I apologise, Mr. For this is indeed the porridge without the oatmeal, or the salt either, by the great Jehoshaphat ! ! By heaven, this is the very essence of fun ! Mark Twain, my boy, look to your laurels ! ! This old buck presses you vurry, vurry hard ! ! " "You a tragedian," he continued betwixt the paroxisms. "Why, man alive, you are the very lowest low comedy, side-splitting funniosity, on the face of the earth."

His laughter irritated me tremendously. "Sir," I said, boiling with righteous indignation, "you have the audacity to call Shakespeare a liar ; and you compare my poems to porridge. I tell you to your face, you are a mendacious liar, a blackguard, a traducer, and a mocker at morality. I would not take an engagement from you at £1,000 a week."

"Splendid ! Capital ! Bravo ! " he roared, as I made for the door. "By thunder, that man will kill me."

"Amen," I replied, as I banged his painted panels, and left the premises.

Shocked and disgusted, but carrying my head erect, as best beseemed one who had scored heavily in the interests of morality, I made for another place of entertainment not far off. I sent no card on this or any subsequent occasion, having now become thoroughly convinced that these cards

J. M. Wallace & Sons
Makers of "Land o' Cakes" Products

Estimates for All Classes of
Catering, Weddings, Dances,
Socials, etc., etc., with pleasure

CATERING DEPT.

STOBSWELL BAKERY

Phone 3824

DUNDEE

Physicians' Prescriptions
ARE ACCURATELY DISPENSED WITH PURE
DRUGS BY

A. Nicol Taylor

DISPENSING AND
FAMILY CHEMIST

41 Dens Road
DUNDEE
Telephone No. 2488

Try CARBERG OINTMENT for Boils, etc.

were intended by the man who printed them for me as a regular " cod," to make people laugh at me. Walking, therefore, right into the vestibule, I saw a man, tall, thin, and sallow, with firmly compressed lips, and wearing a frock coat and silk hat. I accosted him, and asked if I could see the " boss." " You do see him," he drawled. I lifted my hat and said, " Sir, you see before you a tragedian in poor circumstances, anxious to have an opportunity of appearing before an American audience."

" Don't try it, my good man," he answered, piercing me with his eagle eye. " Take my advice, and get over the water again as soon as you can, as the prejudice is so great on this side against British actors that I would to a certainty get my show wrecked right away if any of them appeared on my stage. And I feel certain," he added with a mocking smile, " that you are the last man to contemplate such a catastrophe with equanimity."

" I certainly am, sir. But what am I to do ; I have no money," I replied.

" That's bad," he said ; " but I can't help you in any way. Get your friends on the other side to scrape up the price of your passage. You will never manage to do it yourself in New York. Go straight home, and write to Andrew Carnegie for an organ. They tell me he gives them away for nothing."

" Not to private individuals, sir ; only to churches," I answered. " Mr. Carnegie is a good man and benevolent ; is very willing to help his countrymen ; but, in my opinion, he goes a somewhat strange way about it. We in Scotland have a song about a piper who had a cow, and no food to give her, so he took his pipes and played a tune to the poor famished beast, entitled ' Corn rigs are bonnie.' There are thousands in Scotland at this moment good, honest, virtuous men and women, who, with their children, are at the point of starvation through no fault of their own. Mr. Carnegie's organs will do as much good to them as the piper's tune did to the cow, or as your advice will do to me. Good-morning, sir."

You may wonder why I cut this interview so short. I will tell you. I knew intuitively from the expression of his face that he was a hard, greedy man. I knew that he lied when he told me that there was a prejudice against British artists, as Henry Irving, Dion Boucicault, and all the other stars of our country were always rapturously received in America ; and I know also that he had formed a very poor

opinion of my abilities as an actor, when he suggested I
should take to organ grinding for a livelihood.   Such is my
Sherlock Homes-like power of penetration that I felt that
no succour of any kind was to be expected from this quarter.
So I went home to dinner, and related my adventures.

It was decided that I should tackle the man on the street
with my poems next day.   The place chosen was a back
road in the vicinity of " The Bowery." The first man I
interviewed had a sad expression on his somewhat comely
face.   I held out my " Spittal of Glenshee " poem to him.
He looked at it solemnly, shook his head, and said " Nein,
nein."

I thought he wanted nine copies, and felt quite elated.
I counted them out, and handed them to him, saying " Four
dollars, please " ; but he brushed them aside with the same
" Nein, nein."

I then commenced to read the poem to him, watching
his face all the time.   Ever and anon as I proceeded his
expression grew more and more stolid and impassive ; not a
smile, not a single gleam of intelligence illumined his weather-
beaten face.   I might as well have been reading a chapter
to a horse for all the impression I was making.   The quadruped
would possibly have interpolated in his own way with the
frequency of the man's " Nein, neins " ; but the net results,
so far as it and I were concerned, would have been precisely
the same as I now experienced.   At length a bystander,
who had been attracted to the spot, informed me that he was
a German emigrant newly landed, on which I desisted, and
addressing my informant, said " Will you buy a poem ? "

" No, sir, I would not take one for nothing," he replied.

" It is a splendid work I assure you," I urged.   " It is
' The Spittal of Glenshee,' and only half a dollar."

He snorted indignantly, " Go on ; who are you trying to
get at ? I would not give you half a cent for all the spittals
in New York."

I expect the ignorant fellow thought I referred to expec-
torations, not knowing the difference, not at all anxious to
learn, for he made off with his nose in the air.   The next
I ventured to accost was evidently a red hot Republican, for
he asked me " if I was not ashamed to parade the Royal Arms
of England through the streets of a free country."

" No, sir," I said, " I am a loyal subject of the Queen
of Britain, and will stick to my colours."

" Take my advice, old man," he said not unkindly, " don't

risk your life at this game, or more than one stick may stick
your vaunted colours of red, white, and blue all over your
carcase.   The symbols of tyranny will not go down here,"
he continued earnestly, " unless to be trampled in the gutter.
If your poems are good and anti-monarchical, tear off the
Royal Arms and they'll maybe fetch a cent a piece ; otherwise
if you escape lynching by the mob, it will only be to fall into
the hands of the police on a charge of inciting to riot.   Of
course, you can please yourself, boss, it's nothing to me ; but
my straight advice to you is to show no more of them in
this country.   I like to see a plucky man, but I reckon it's
going a bit too strong to risk your life for a cent or two."

" A what ? " I cried.   " My price for each poem is half
a dollar."

" Half a dollar ! " he shouted.   " Are you mad ; if
you're not, I'll lay a bet you don't sell a single copy between
now and the day of judgment," and he passed on without
exhibiting the slightest curiosity as to the nature of their
contents.

On turning to go home it began to snow very heavily,
so that by the time I reached my attic I presented the
appearance of a regular Father Christmas.   I did not sleep
that night, the cold was so intense ; this and the terror I was
in owing to the things that Republican had told me kept me
very wide awake ; and to crown all, I was called at six o'clock
next morning to break sticks and sweep away the snow.
Oh, heavens, to think of it !   A duly ordained poet a hewer
of wood and a shoveller of snow.

Every day for a fortnight I tramped the length and breadth
of New York seeking anything to do, but no one would
listen to me or give me a single red cent.   I do not understand
the American people at all.   My poems did not interest
them in the slightest.   Anyone I accosted simply passed on
without a word, good or bad.   My isolation was painfully
complete.   I was not sneered at or despised ; I was not made
the victim of horse play.   I almost wished I had been ;
anything in the world rather than to be ignored.   I was
absolutely helpless and useless, fighting the wind and beating
my hands against unresisting air.   Some treated me as a
lunatic, others as a mendicant, but nobody ever dreamed of
discussing the point.   Oh, the utter desolation of it.

I used to envy the poet Homer his exemption from the
striking attentions which had fallen so plentifully to my lot.
I now recant that envy, and pity the poor old soul from the

bottom of a fellow-feeling heart, for I have now come to the conclusion that any sort of attentions are preferable to this cold American indifference.

In Dundee I was dead value for something like a " bob a bruise." Now I actually felt that I would gladly have had a few of them at a considerably reduced figure.

Do you wonder then that all my energies were now directed to getting back to Dundee as fast as possible ? The first step was to write to Mr. A. C. Lamb asking him, for God's sake, to redeem the captivity of his humble servant according to promise. This I did, posted it, and waited. In due course I called at the shipping office of the Anchor Line, to which address I had instructed Mr. Lamb to reply. I asked Mr. Stewart, the manager, if there was any letter for me.

" Oh, yes ; it's all right," was the cheering answer. " I had a cable from Mr. Lamb to give you a second cabin passage back and six pounds.

This I got half in American money and half in British, along with my ticket for the same vessel (the *Circassian*) as I had come out in. I nearly fainted with joy, a most unusual predicament for me.

In due time I arrived in Dundee, having occupied my time during the passage to Glasgow in writing a poem of fifteen stanzas, which will live, if for nothing else than the faithful picture it gives of New York and my feelings at leaving it. It is too long to insert here, but I give you the four concluding stanzas :—

> And there are also ten thousand rum sellers there,
> Oh, wonderful to think of, I do declare ;
> To accommodate the people of New York therein,
> And encourage them to commit all sorts of sin.
>
> And on the Sabbath day ye will see many a man
> Going for beer with a big tin can,
> And seems proud to be seen carrying home the beer,
> To treat his neighbours and his family dear.
>
> Then at night numbers of people dance and sing,
> Making the walls of their homes to ring
> With their songs and dancing on Sabbath night ;
> Which I witnessed with disgust, and fled from the sight.
>
> And with regard to New York and the sights I did see,
> Believe me, I never saw such sights in Dundee ;

> And the morning I sailed from the city of New York,
> My heart it felt as light as a cork.

This, my dear friends in its entirety, is one of the finest poems in the English language.

I Take Glasgow by Storm

> " Where hath Scotland found her glory ?
>   Whence her mighty enterprise ?
> Let St. Mungo tell the story,
>   For in her the answer lies."— *Old Song*.

On landing at Glasgow, I had some time to wait for a train to Dundee. This gave me a long wished for opportunity of seeing the sights of St. Mungo, which are really much better worth a visit than I had imagined. When I began to write uninspired poetry, as you are aware, I included Glasgow in the scope of my themes, a proof that my spirit sometimes wandered west ; but when I wrote that " the prettiest river that ever I saw was Glasgow on the Clyde," it was merely a poet's licence, and a proof of my unlimited imagination— a faculty which the vulgar construe vulgarly.

For, save for my visit to America, my bodily peregrinations had hitherto been exclusively confined to the east of Scotland, the glories of which had so filled my mind to the exclusion of all others, that I thought I had seen and heard all that was worth seeing and hearing, at least in the land of my birth.

I was like the trout who lived in a three-acre pond—very difficult to persuade that there was anything of any consequence outside of my severely proscribed limits. America had opened my eyes in one way—it showed me that there were larger ponds than the one I grew up in, but infested with pike, who monopolised all the food, in which I myself was catalogued as one of the choicest morsels.

In Glasgow—to drop metaphor—I found a live and let live spirit, a feeling of reverence for the muses, which was carried to a very pleasant excess in their treatment of me as the embodiment of poetry. It is to hug a miserable delusion to believe that the gentlemen live in Edinburgh and the parvenues in Glasgow. This idea, owing to my experience, is now completely exploded. I must confess, however, that my conception of Glasgow before this visit was founded and fostered through the envy-begotten ideas of Edinburgh, to the effect that the sole aim and object of its inhabitants was to amass money.

The merchant princes of St. Mungo—and I speak now from practical experience and unbounded powers of observation are cultured gentlemen in the highest sense of the term, which simply means a due consideration for the feelings of others, a commodity they could export to the east with as little loss to themselves and as much advantage to the importers, as they do everything else which is for the benefit of mankind generally.

How strange it seems that a man of my forethought and discernment should always run up against such marvellous surprises. I feared and trembled to go to Perth ; the same feeling pervaded me on taking my journey to Inverness. In both cases I was agreeably disappointed ; but, as Oliver Cromwell said about the battle of Dunbar, Glasgow was " my crowning mercy." It all happened in this wise. Amongst the many places of interest I visited was the world-famed and palatial warehouse of Mann, Byars, & Co., in whose employ was an old Dundee friend and admirer. He introduced me to the heads of the various departments, and they were so struck with my appearance and general attainments as to resolve there and then to get up a select entertainment for me on the following evening.

They sent round the hat amongst themselves, and collected as much as kept me in comfort for the night, and something over.

The place selected was in Glassford Street, and when I appeared on the scene next evening at eight o'clock, the hall was filled with the *elite* of the city. The chairman, who was introduced to me, was a Baronet and an M.P., whose name I forget. He was a powerful man, whose corporeal proportions were conceived on a generous scale. He commenced by reading letters of apology from the Lord Provost and other magnates of the city. The Russian Ambassador, Count Kutiswartzoff, a distinguished man of letters and a great poet in his own country, also sent an apology, expressed in Russian, to say how sorry he was not to have seen and heard me, or possibly to have been allowed to touch the hem of my garment, in order to carry the emanating virtue to Kamskatka, a place of sin and degradation, to which he was bound on the morrow, and to whence its efficacy might have been transmitted through his unworthy medium.

" Tell Mr. M'Gonagall from me," he added, " to persevere in his great and holy mission, because nothing but the emanations from great poets will conduce to the healing of the nations and hasten the millennium.   My friend, Baron Ballyrot, of the German Embassy, has expressed a strong desire to be present at your interesting levee, and though he unfortunately knows no English, yet being the greatest pantomimic and thought reader in the universe, he will be able to report the proceedings to me with an accuracy which is simply marvellous.   To him, therefore, I commend you. Kindly let him have a seat on the platform."

This letter was handed to me, and then shown round the company.   I have it still, but as it is written in tea box characters, I am sorry I cannot reproduce it here.

The chairman's address was a flattering appreciation of my powers as a poet and my modesty as a man.   He told the audience in terms more eloquent than I can convey that there, as I sat in the garb of old Gaul, I was a sight that the very blind would rejoice to see, the greatest Scottish poet of all time, and the unique product of a century.

When the chairman sat down, a gentleman at the back of the hall, after thanking me for shedding the light of my countenance amongst them, stated that the letter of apology from the Russian Ambassador had suggested an idea.   " It is all very well," he continued, " for the chairman and gentlemen on the platform to be able to touch the hem of the poet's garments, and revel in what the distinguished Count so happily characterised as ' the poetical emanation ' ; but," he added, " as those in the back of the hall were quite as desirous of indulging in the moral cleansing inhalation, he suggested that the poet be requested to hand round his bonnet."

To this I readily agreed, and it was impressive to witness with what reverence they passed it carefully from one to another.   Presently a shout arose, " We want more ; send round his coat."   To this I also agreed, though with great reluctance, as my nether garments had been last laundried at New York.   Soon again, however, came the demand in strident tones from all parts of the house, " More, more ; we feel better already.   Send round your vest."   After some persuasion from the chairman and sundry quick nods of assent from the Baron, I at length complied, and was at once complimented by the former on being a perfect presentiment of the " Dugal Cratur," which he explained was the most popular stage character in Glasgow.

This mollified me somewhat, though the position struck me as being a little grotesque, considering my status as a

For - -

Romarys Famous
Tunbridge Wells Biscuits

Water.   Digestive.   Ginger Nuts.
Wheaten Water.   Cheese Gaufrets.   Celery Sticks, etc.

Woods Famous
Perth Wine Biscuits

" Tiptree " Famous
Jams, Jellies, Marmalades and Conserves

Tiptree Scarlet Strawberry.   Morello Cherry.
Tiptree Sweetheart Strawberry.   Red Currant.
Philippine Plum with Kernel.   Black Currant.

GO TO - -
W. MILLAR & SONS
75 High Street   :   :   DUNDEE

poet and an honoured guest. After shivering till the vest went round, to my inexpressible surprise and horror, the house rose again " en masse," and shouted vociferously " The kilt, the kilt ; send round the poet's kilt."

This roused me at once to prompt action, and springing to my feet, I paused for a brief space until the cries had somewhat subsided, and then in the well-known stentorian tones in which I have electrified thousands in the rôle of Macbeth, I arrested attention by that glorious outburst, " ' I dare all that may become a man, who does more is none.' Gentlemen, I appeared before you as a poet and tragedian. At your earnest request I then assumed the character of Highland ghillie ; but I most emphatically draw the line at playing Adam before the Fall in a chillier climate than Eden." At which the Baron shouted " Bravo ! bravissimo ! " and clapped his hands, which emitted sounds like pistol shots. Truly a rare judge of histrionic ability is the Baron !

Seeing I was incensed, and backed up by the Teuton, they cheered me to the echo, and one of the audience leaped on to the platform, and facing me in the chair which I had resumed, bowed profoundly to me, and began to sing a long song with a longer refrain about a miner's daughter named Clementine, who met a watery grave through the inordinate length of her feet. But the music and the rhythm were so sweet, melodious, and haunting that I, like King Saul under the influence of David's harp, felt instantly soothed, and began to keep time with my feet to its melodious cadences. In fact, if I had only had my clothes on I would have been perfectly happy.

At length, so pathetic was the story, so entrancing the refrain, that the entire audience, first bowing reverentially towards me, took up the theme lustily, and repeated the fascinating strain over and over again, until six or eight of them, unable to contain themselves any longer, joined the solo singer on the platform, where they clasped hands and jingo-ringed round my chair, singing louder and louder until all traces of righteous wrath were completely exorcised, and I joined heartily in bemoaning the luckless fate of the charming Clementine.

> She drove her ducklings to the water
> Every morning just at nine ;
> But her feet caught in a slipper,
> And she plunged into the brine.

O, my darling ! O, my darling !
O, my darling, Clementine !
Thou art lost, and gone for ever,
Dreadful sorry, Clementine.

I would I knew the author. What a collaboration he and I could make. But whether I ever meet him in the flesh or not, these words of his will haunt my soul and ring in my ears till my dying day ; and from henceforth that pathetic and swinging dance with its weird-like melody will ever be associated in my mind with the witches' cauldron in Macbeth, only, instead of gruesome curiosities flung into it by " black and midnight hags," there would be the jingle of coins unstintedly rattled into the sacred circle by a crowd of well-dressed, high-souled merchant princes of Glasgow.

For the first time in my life the usual order of things was completely reversed. I was the entertained, and my audience the entertainers. It was, as I said, a unique experience, and yet I felt not the slightest desire for it to be otherwise, and between laughter and tears could have sat and sung the whole night through. But the chairman courteously reminded me that the company was impatient for pabulum of a more soul-satisfying nature, and would now hear the gospel according to M'Gonagall at my earliest convenience. This I at once proceeded to impart in such a feast of reason and a flow of soul, partly from my own works and partly from Shakespeare, that never in the annals of this or any other city was such a rational and instructive evening spent.

Even the big Baron nodded his head again in evident approval, and so well pleased was the entire company that the chairman asked if I would have anything on the following night, a question which elicited the remark from me that I could scarcely have less on any night than I had at the moment, a witticism which, amid roars of laughter, brought me the missing " togs " at once.

Whether that vast and aristocratic gathering felt better for my emanations or not, I most assuredly felt better of theirs ; and the sum of £4 15s., added to the balance of Mr. A. C. Lamb's superb donation, enabled me with a light heart and a heavy purse, accompanied by neither wounds, bruises, or insults, to chronicle a record event in my career and a chapter virtually free from lamentations.

In honour of so unique an event I threw my whole soul

into the composition of a poem on my impressions of Glasgow, which I append with the simple remark that if the reader gets no more for his shilling than this and the cover of the book, it would save him a lot of reading, and give him the best value to be had on earth for the money.

O, beautiful city of Glasgow, which stands on the river Clyde,
How happy should the people be which in ye reside ;
Because it is the most enterprising city of the present day,
Whatever anybody else may say.
The ships which lie at the Broomilaw are most beautiful to see,
They are bigger and best than any in Dundee ;
Likewise the municipal buildings, most gorgeous to be seen,
Near to Ingram Street, and not far from Glasgow Green.
Then the warehouses are filled from the floor to the topmost
With goods, which brings Glasgow money and glory ;   [storey
And the men who own them are most liberal, I do declare,
Because I got money from them when there.
O' wonderful city of Glasgow, with your triple expansion
    engines,
At the making of which your workmen get many singeins ;
Also the deepening of the Clyde, most marvellous to behold,
Which cost much money, be it told.
Then there is a grand picture gallery,
Which the keepers thereof are paid a very large salary ;
Therefore, citizens of Glasgow, do not fret or worry,
For there is nothing like it in all Edinburgh.
And the happiest night I ever spent,
Was in Glasgow, where I got as much as pay my rent
From your merchant princes most fine,
Who likewise sang a song to me called Clementine ;
Which was most beautiful to hear, also a dance
Round and round, all singing at once ;
And the treatment I got in Glasgow, I must confess,
Was better even than Inverness.
Oh, beautiful city of Glasgow, I must conclude my lay,
By calling thee the greatest city of the present day ;
For your treatment of me was by no means curlish,
Therefore I say, " Let Glasgow flourish."

You will observe that in this beautiful and exhaustive, descriptive poem I have omitted all reference to the stripping episode, because the poem, which is built to last longer than the prose on which it is set, will be read centuries after the autobiography has been consigned to forgetfulness.

D

'Twas on the 16th of October, in the year 1894,
I was invited to Inverness, not far from the sea shore,
To partake of a banquet prepared by the " Heather Blend
Gentlemen who honoured me without any hubbub.   [Club,"
The   banquet   was   held   in   the   Gillion   Hotel,
And the landlord, Mr. McPherson, treated me right well ;
Also the servant maids were very kind to me,
Especially the girl that polished my boots most beautiful to see.
The banquet consisted of roast beef, potatoes, and red wine,
Also hare soup and sherry and grapes most fine,
Also baked pudding and apples lovely to be seen,
Also rich sweet milk and delicious cream.
Mr. Gossip, a noble Highlander, acted as chairman
And when the banquet was finished the fun began,
And I was requested to give a public entertainment,
Which I gave, and it pleased them to their hearts content.
And for my entertainment they did me well reward,
By titling me there the " Heather Blend Club " bard
Likewise I received an illuminated address,
Also a purse of silver, I honestly confess.
Oh, magnificent city of Inverness,
And your beautiful river, I must confess,
With its lovely scenery on each side,
Would be good for one's health there to reside.
There the blackbird and mavis together doth sing,
Making the woodlands with their echoes ring
During the months of July, May, and June,
When the trees and the shrubberies are in full bloom.
And to see the river Ness rolling smoothly along,
Together with the blackbird's musical song,
When the sun shines bright in the month of May,
Will help to drive dull care away.
And Macbeth's castle is grand to be seen,
Situated on Castle Hill, which is beautiful and green ;
'Twas there Macbeth lived in days of old,
And a very great tyrant he was, I am told.
I wish the members of the " Heather Blend Club " every success!
Hoping God will prosper them and bless ;
Long may Dame Fortune smile upon them,
For all of them I have met are kind gentlemen.
And in praise of them, I must say
I never received better treatment in my day
Than I received from my admirers in bonnie Inverness,
This upon my soul and conscience I do confess.

I am made a Knight of the White Elephant
of Burmah

> Grassmarket born, Grassmarket reared,
>   And yet he rose to be
> A bard who nearly twice appeared
>   At Courts of Royalty.—*Court Circular.*

The venue of my life story is now changed farther away than even New York, to the land of burning suns, to the country of the elephant and the ruby, to the Andaman Islands, which are under the sway of that dusky, but powerful potentate, King Thebaw of Burmah. 'Tis a wonderful story, how our names came to be linked together, and reads more like a *Monte Cristo* romance than the plain, unvarnished truth, which it undoubtedly is.

King Thebaw then sat in state in one of these islands. He sat on his gold and ivory throne. At either side of him was a huge elephant, life size, cast in solid silver. Right over his head gleamed a canopy of gold, surmounted by a wondrous peacock, whose body and tail were studded with diamonds and rubies as big as French beans. His royal robes shimmered with oriental pearls, like the firmament on a starry night.

The splendour of the scene beggars all description. The walls of the throne room in which he held his Court were of the purest white marble, relieved with tiers of vivid green, gothic shaped niches all round, from the topaz inlaid floor to the massive gold dome, so richly set with emeralds. In many of these niches were statues of men in gold, mounted on silver elephants. These statues were those of the Knights of the White Elephant of Burmah since the flood, an Order open to merit alone wherever found. In former times these niches were strictly reserved for the poets of Burmah ; but the rule was relaxed in consequence of a fear which had for some generations possessed the Rulers of Burmah of not being able to fill all the blanks with native talent before the year of our Lord 2000. This limit was set by the founder of the Order, with the prophetic intimation if it was exceeded, with one single niche left untenanted, the Empire of Burmah would crumble into oblivion.

The hall was thronged by men gorgeously attired, of every nationality under heaven. It was the annual meeting of the Knights of the Holy Order, convened to elect a worthy occupant for one of these much coveted recesses in the wall. Right opposite the king, at the extreme end of the hall, stood another throne, scarcely less magnificent than the one on which Thebaw sat. This was and is the chair of the Holy Order, in which the duly elected knights—men of outstanding ability in the realms of poetry—are in the fulness of time installed with all the rights and ceremonies prescribed by the illustrious founder.

For seven long years none had been found worthy of instalment, or else were in some way or other unable to fulfil the strictly-imposed conditions, and so the king was sad, sullen, and morose. The harpers who harped on silver harps, and the trumpeters who trumpeted on golden trumpets, tried in vain to bring a smile to the sulky monarch's face. Let them play their liveliest music, the muscles on that mahogany frontispiece would not relax to the tenth of a hairsbreadth, and the only response elicited from it was a sigh and a groan, and a doleful " Ah, me." They varied the tune a dozen times, but all to no purpose, the stolid look became more impassive still, and a fearful funereal silence fell on all around.

At length a Scotsman, Macdonald by name, high in the Order, and Poet Laureate of Burmah, was seen to whisper in the ear of the chief of the musicians. That functionary, with a wave of his hand, at once stilled the orchestra, then he in turn whispered something in the ear of each bandsman. After a longish pause, the music struck up again, and a sudden transformation took place. You have seen an icebound pool, suddenly kissed by a genial thaw, break up in wrinkles and tears. This is a weak metaphor, and a feeble indication of what happened to the royal face. First he smiled—the first smile he had smiled for nearly two years— then he roared in a perfect paroxism of laughter, eventually rising on his throne and dancing like one possessed, the tears of mirth rolling in torrents down his ebony cheeks.

" Stop ! stop ! " he roared to the chief musician. " Stop or I shall go mad with joy. In the name of all the Burmese gods at once, what tune is this ? "

Then the Poet Laureate opened his mouth and replied, " Sire,"

> " It is the ' Rattling Boy from Dublin town,'
> By a British bard of great renown."

" Bring him forth," was the royal mandate, " and see if we cannot get him to fill at least two niches ; but, meantime," he continued, " let our chief singer, sing me the words

of this all too fascinating melody." At this command the
Poet Laureate, first bowing to the king, and saying, " Sire,
I prefer to do justice to this myself," he nodded to the conductor, and straightway broke forth, to the accompaniment
of the harps, the trumpets, and the cymbals—

> " I'm the rattling boy from Dublin town,
> I courted a girl called Biddy Brown ;
> Her eyes they were as black as sloes,
> She had black hair and an aquiline nose.
>
>> Wack fal the dooral, ooral, ido,
>> Wack fal the dooral, ooral, aa',
>> Wack fal the dooral, ooral, ido,
>> Wack fal the dooral, ooral, aa'.
>
> Now Biddy Brown, from County Down,
> Was the biggest decayver in the town,
> For all the time she was coortin' me
> She was goin' about wid Barney M'Ghee.
>> Wack fal the dooral, &c.
>
> Till one fine day it came to pass
> I met Bould Barney wid my lass ;
> Wid my darling shileleagh I knocked him down—
> For I'm the rattling boy from Dublin town.
>> Wack fal the dooral, &c.
>
> Said Barney M'Ghee unto me,
> I must cave in, I plainly see ;
> So take you back your Biddy Brown,
> The greatest decayver in Dublin town.
>> Wack fal the dooral, &c.
>
> Then Biddy wid the aquiline nose,
> Punched poor Barney's as he rose ;
> ' Farewell,' she cried, ' ye cowardly clown,
> I'm off wid my boy from Dublin town.'
>> Wack fal the dooral, &c."

And the Poet Laureate sang, and the orchestra played,
and the king danced, and ever and anon as the music stopped
or Macdonald paused for breath, the king shouted impatiently,
" Go on, go on." Never was such a lively or a more exhausting
jig danced, sung, or played since time began. All this was
duly minuted in the records of the Order, and the scene
therein described as the " Dance of the Gods." At length

Don't be vague — ask for **Haig**

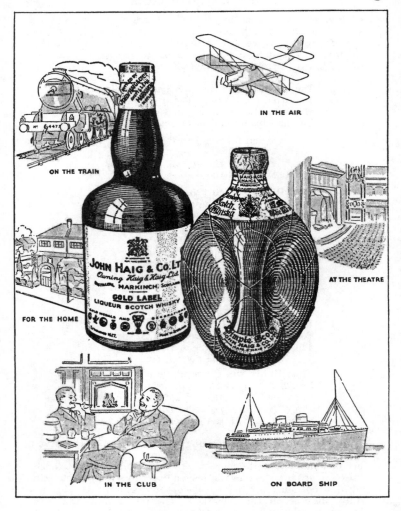

NO FINER WHISKY GOES INTO ANY BOTTLE

McQueen 1524

the king, thoroughly tired out, had only strength enough to exclaim, " Let him fill three niches," when he collapsed.

On regaining consciousness, it was fully explained to him that the bard lived in Perth, Scotland, and a committee was appointed to draw up an intimation of his election to the Holy Order of the Knights of the White Elephant of Burmah, which intimation duly arrived at South Street towards the end of January, 1895.

In this letter—which was of enormous size, and addressed Sir Wm. Topaz MacGonagall—was a real silver elephant, attached to a green silk ribbon, which I understand is the insignia of the knighthood. The letter itself is as follows :—

Court of King Thebaw,
Andaman Islands,

December 2nd, 1894.

Dear and Most Highly
Honoured Sir,

Having the honour to belong to the same Holy Order as yourself, I have been requested to inform you by His Royal Highness King Thebaw that you, after satisfactory examination through the medium of one of your own immortal songs, have been duly elected a Grand Knight of the Most Holy Order of the White Elephant of Burmah (three niches), and that henceforth you are to be known and respected as Sir William Topaz M'Gonagall, G.K.H.O.W.E.B. That you will consent to accept of the high honour now offered to you is the wish nearest to the hearts not only of the king himself, but also of all your countrymen here in the East, who will never cease to pray that you may be long spared to enrich British literature by your grand and thrilling works, the power and pathos of which have been so exhaustively tested at this Court.

Should you see fit to do the ancient Kingdom of Burmah the honour of accepting the ribbon of its highest award, you will kindly pay its capital a visit at your earliest convenience, to be duly installed in the holy chair of the Knights of the above Order, from which you will be expected, according to the custom of the holy fraternity, to address a manifesto to the whole world.

King Thebaw, who has been terribly impressed by your extreme modesty, will not risk insulting your sensitive feelings by offering you any filthy lucre, more especially as the shield and motto of the Order is a white elephant wading to the belly in gold, with the legend " Wisdom above Riches."

At the same time, as a signal mark of unusual appreciation, he is sending you by an early steamer the biggest white elephant in all Burmah, as a living and standing reminder to you of the colossal nature of the honour he has bestowed upon you.

I have the honour to be, most noble and illustrious sir, your most humble brother in the fraternity of the poets,

C. MACDONALD, K.O.W.E.B.,
Poet Laureate of Burmah.

By order of His Royal Highness the King.

TOPAZ GENERAL.
TOPAZ MINISTER.
SECRETARY OF STATE.
HOLDER OF SEALS.
KEEPER OF THE WHITE ELEPHANT.

P.S.—Kindly address all communications *re* this and other matters of State to Sylvester Smith, Esq., Burmese Chargé d'Affaires, 21, Gardners' Crescent, Edinburgh.

This letter filled me at once with the keenest pleasure and the greatest consternation—pleasure to have my services recognised by a knighthood, and absolute terror at the coming of that enormous brute, which, even if carriage paid, would devour in an hour all that I could earn in a month, and keep me in perpetual starvation.

Thus my pleasures by a perverse fate have always been alloyed. Besides, where was I to keep the monster ? If it attempted to reach the garret in South Street, at every step the stairs would go like rotten girds, and the damages I would have to pay would totally overwhelm me. If I led it about the streets the police would interfere, and no stable in Perth has a doorway sufficiently big to admit it. I do not know the value of such an animal ; but this I do know, that motto of the Order or no motto, I would much rather have had half of the gold it is depicted as wading among than twenty elephants. Of course, I dare not say this to Thebaw, or he might deem me unworthy of the knighthood.

To such a state of nerves was I reduced that, sinful man that I am, I prayed fervently that the ship which conveyed it to me would become a total wreck. Of course, I would have preferred that the brute should jump overboard and be drowned ; but if that was not to be, I was prepared, rather than face that elephant in Perth, to read with equanimity the account of the whole bally lot, captain, crew, and passengers, being engulfed in the bosom of any sea, red, black, or white, so long as the elephant went with them.

That night I dreamed a dream, and the interpretation thereof was not such as to tax the powers of a Daniel. I dreamed I lay, in the brilliant sun of a July day, in a lovely meadow dotted with daisies and buttercups, that I was being crowned with garlands and loaded with honours, and acclaimed as the king of poetry, and so loud were the plaudits of the people that I could not hear the stealthy approach of a gigantic form, which anon assumed the shape of an enormous elephant, which presently lay down beside me, imprisoning my legs tightly under its huge haunches. By and bye it rolled more and more over me, till its weight was so oppressive as to threaten me with complete annihilation. I wriggled in a vain endeavour to escape, only to find my face in close proximity to its glaring eyes and terrible tusks ready to gore my breathless body. At this I awoke in an agony of fear and sweat, and narrated the dream to my alarmed spouse.

" Ah, Willie," she said, " is this no most mighty ? It's the worst calamity ever cam' ower you ! A sham cheque disna' eat onything, it's juist a ' cod ' an' dune we'd, an' a pepperin' at an entertainment cleans aff or heals in a fortnicht ; but this brute—an' they say they live 300 year—'ill be a bonny millstane roond yer neck day an' nicht a' yer life, unless ye pushion it as sune's it comes."

" That's all very well," I said ; " but what would the king think ? He might revoke my knighthood."

" Weel, weel," she said, " juist lat him du'd ; there's nae siller comin' we'd, an' if that's the case, he micht as weel gi'en ye a nicht-cape as a nicht-hood, an' a hantle better too, for the ane wad be some use, and the ither, as far as I can see, michty little."

What was the use of arguing with a woman possessed of ideas like these, so, with a deep drawn sigh, I was once more flung on my own resources. These inspired me to write at once to Mr. Sylvester Smith, in Edinburgh, as follows :—

SOUTH STREET,
PERTH.

January, 31, 1895.

Dear Sir,—The knighthood is to hand. Tell the king from me I thank him with my whole soul, and will write him in due course ; but for heaven's sake tell him to stop that elephant he is sending me anywhere between Burmah and Perth. If you do not, my blood lies at your door, for the moment it reaches Perth my life is not worth an hour's purchase.—Yours truly and in trepidation,

WILLIAM M'GONAGALL, Poet.

D*

In due time I was plunged into the third heaven of delight by a telegram from Edinburgh, brief, but blissful—

From Smith, Edinburgh.

To M'Gonagall, Perth.

" Elephant stopped in Suez Canal."

I rushed upstairs to my wife as fast as I could from the post office, where I got it, and entering the house breathless, I shouted, flourishing the wire, " Hurrah ! hurrah ! the elephant has been stopped in the Suez Canal."

" Dear me, Willie," ejaculated my astonished spouse. " Dear me, what an enormous brute that soo must hae been to swallow an elephant ; nae winder it stuck in the brute's gullet or canal, as they ca' it. Lat it get oot o'd the best wey it can, it's better there than in Perth ony wey."

You can easily conceive the difficulty of enlightening one who, in culinary and general domestic arrangements is all that could be desired, but whose knowledge of the great waterway was so evidently limited.

As I learned afterwards, the moving mountain was booked at Burmah *carriage forward.* You can form some little idea of the immense load which was lifted from my chest, more especially when I tell you that the Khedive of Egypt, into whose hands it eventually fell, had to pay £200 for food and carriage, and to name it " M'Gonagall " before he was allowed to touch it. Relieved from this incubus I breathed freely, so freely that existence, even in poverty and as far in debt as they would allow me, was positively delicious. It was only occasionally in dreams after this that I suffered from " Elephantophobia." These fears, however, entirely vanished in waking moments, and I wrote a letter to the king, which ran thus :—

South Street,
Perth.

March 10*th*, 1895.

To His august Majesty the King of Burmah.

Sire,—This comes greeting from your humble slave, the Poet M'Gonagall, on whom your Majesty has vouchsaved the light of your countenance by creating him a worshipful Knight after the Order of the White Elephant, whose motto, I am proud to note, is " Wisdom above Riches." May both be multiplied to your Royal Highness until your storehouses of each are abundantly filled.

In the case of your humble slave, nature and circumstances have made a very one-sided arrangement as regards those two precious commodities ; for at the present I can say without fear of contradiction, if the wisdom of your humble slave were not above the riches he possesses, he would indeed be, what the whole world knows he is not, the veriest idiot in the universe. I am not complaining, only had it been otherwise I would not have been forced to forgo the greatest pleasure the world has ever dangled before my wistful eyes. I refer to your Royal Highness's unique and powerful present, which I did not countermand for any other reason save that I could neither pay carriage on it or feed it any way, let alone in accordance with the manner I would desire to do, for the reverence and love which I bear for the august donor, whose large-hearted benevolence to the poor and needy is well known all over the civilised globe.

> Your Highness's early reply,
> Will raise its recipient heavens high."

Your abject and grateful slave,

Sir WILLIAM TOPAZ M'GONAGALL, G.K.H.O.W.E.B.

This, as was fitting, was the first time I signed my new title, not excepting my letter to the Charge d'Affaires, to whom under cover I sent the foregoing ; but I never received a reply owing, I understand, to a revolution which took place in Burmah in consequence, I am informed, of the fact that a three-niched honour—the first for 1,000 years—had been conferred on a foreigner.

This, though excessively disappointing, was nothing exceptional to my usual luck, and so, with an empty purse, an empty stomach, and a no less empty title, I William M'Gonagall, to be known henceforth as Sir William Topaz M'Gonagall, left Perth, and took up my abode in Edinburgh.

The last few years of the Poet's life were spent in Edinburgh where he continued to hawk his wares, and as inevitably happened, irrepressible studentdom got on his track and one of his last public appearances took place in a hotel adjoining "The Gaiety" theatre where the late Sir E. Moss started that famous string of music halls associated with his name. As was usual, pandemonium reigned and finished up as the poet remarked "with making gingerbread on his face," but that he was quite able to stand a few rotten eggs for five bob.

" Sic transit gloria mundi."

"Age cannot wither, nor custom stale"

The Dundee Eastern Co-Operative Society, Limited

Because indispensable to the well-being of the Community, its roots firmly planted in its soil, it is perennially

Fresh and Active,

growing in popularity, and increasing in strength as the years roll on.

In value unsurpassed,
In service unexcelled ;
In quality it leads the way,
By every test upheld.

Dividend paid on All Purchases

Therefore—

The Slogan for all time is,

SHOP at the CO-OP.

W. M. Crooks, *Gen. Manager.*

Dundee Stage-Door Comedy

(*Dundee Courier and Advertiser, March 6th* 1933)

ASS BEATS FOREIGN LEGION—REFUSES TO JOIN " DESERT SONG "

There are " silly asses " who make fame and fortune on the stage. This is the tale of an ass which refused to go on the stage for love or money.

No reflection is intended on any member of the Dundee Amateur Operatic Society when it is stated that this ass had a chance of being a member of the cast.

This is how it was. The society is producing to-night *The Desert Song*, and they needed a donkey—a real live donkey. Camels are not the only beasts of burden associated with the desert. Donkeys are useful on the sandy desert as well as the sandy beach.

Yesterday was the final rehearsal, and final rehearsals have to be the real thing. So the donkey was brought round to the King's Theatre to make his debut.

CHOICE OF TWO

To be accurate, two donkeys were brought round by the owner. One was very docile, but he had a slight fault. He always lay down whenever anyone got on his back.

This was no good to the society, as the comedy parts had already been allocated. A serious donkey was what was wanted. The docile donkey was returned with thanks, and the services of the other one were enlisted.

All was well. The rehearsal could proceed. So thought the society.

The donkey thought otherwise. He had grave objections to going on the stage. He proved the truth of the old adage. " You can take a donkey to the stage door, but you cannot make him enter."

For three solid hours, actors and stage hands tried to cajole, shove or otherwise force him over the threshold, but that donkey was not having any. Stage life, he let them understand, never did have any attraction for him.

Had he been miraculously endowed, as was Balaam's

ass, he would have told them something. Being an ordinary
ass, he simply stopped dead and let them shove.

Meanwhile the rehearsal was being held up. The actor
who should have been intimately associated with the donkey
in the play came on the scene to see what had come over
his friend. He tried kindness. This took the form of sugar
knots and carrots, delicacies understood to be irresistible.

Nothing doing. The donkey was not to be an actor either
for a piece of sugar or a carrot.

A sort of tug-of-war was then tried. One man grabbed
the donkey's ears, which are fine things for gripping. Another
man got hold of its tail. They both pulled heartily, but the
tail won.

Then a Foreign Legion officer, complete with spurs, got
on the job. He cantered the animal up and down, and the
donkey enjoyed it. Every time he got to the stage door
he stopped dead, and even a little touch with the spurs had
no effect.

No *Desert Song* for him. He warbled a few notes at intervals
to show them what he could do if he cared.

The stage doorkeeper had a brain-wave. Stage doorkeepers
are naturally a versatile people. What was wrong with
the donkey, he opined, was that it did not like the look of
the flagstones at the entrance.

So he fetched a carpet and laid it over the flagstones.
The donkey exhibited no emotion at the Sir Walter Raleigh
stunt. It remained indifferent.

A corps of Foreign Legionaries tried their luck, but all
they succeeded in doing was to add to the amusement of the
crowd, who were having a most enjoyable P.S.A. If the
crowd inside the theatre enjoy themselves as much as the
crowd outside did, then the society is going to do great
business.

Finally, they gave it up. The rehearsal went on without
a donkey.

But it's all right. The show will go on just as well without
the donkey. The society has got a pony for the job.

Mr Robin Nothgiel to Mr. Foo Foozle

MY DEAR FOOZLE,
      Have you ever heard of " Spunk Janet," the " spae wife ? "
If not, I must tell you that she lives in Cathro's Close, narrow
of the Murraygate, and drives a brisk trade in manufacturing

spunks and telling fortunes. Janet, they say, has dealings with the powers of darkness, and in her magic chamber gets glimpses into the time to come. Her principal customers are old maids, wanton widows, and impatient lasses, the fruits of whose faith keep Janet's "pot boilin'," as the charge made by her for a sicht into the future or a love charm is the "even halfcroon." Janet does not need to advertise her business ; her trade is a flourishing one, being founded on that very old and useful principle of our nature called by general consent "Gullibility." A few nights ago, a love-sick maiden from "Pill Row," alias South Tay Street, called on Janet ; whose case, and the very wise counsel tendered to her by Janet, I have embodied in the following verses, and if you think them worthy of being preserved amongst your "Literary Scraps," which you delight in reading to your numerous friends when discussing a "bowl o' punch" or a glass "o' guid Glenlivet," I shall look on it as a favourable manifestation of your wondrous critical sagacity. I am,

My dear Foozle,
With profound reverence, your ardent admirer,
Robin Nothgiel.

Spunk Janet's Cure for Love.

I've vowed to forget him again and again,
  But vows are as licht as the air is, I trow,
For something within me aye comes wi' a sten'
  And dunts on my heart till I gie up the vow.

I gaed to Spunk Janet, the spaewife, yestreen—
  I've often heard folk o' her wisdom approve—
Quoth she, " It's your fortune you're wantin', I ween ? "
  " Na ! Janet," quoth I, " will ye cure me o' love ? "

" I'll try it," quoth she, " say awa' wi' your tale,
  And tell me the outs and the ins o' it a' ;
Does love mak' ye lichtsome, or does't mak' ye wail ?
  Ye see, lass, I ken it does ane o' thae twa."

" Aweel then, to tell ye the truth o' it, Janet,
  There's sometimes I'm clean overflowin' wi' glee,
And ither times, woman, I'm no fit to stan' it,
  Ye'd think I wad greet out the sicht o' my ee'.

But then there's the laddie, I never can get him,
  And here am I ready and willin' to pay,
Gin ye'll play some cantrip to mak' me forget him—
  The thochts o' him deave me by nicht and by day."

" I'll e'en try my skill on 't," quoth Janet, " I shall,
  The cost o' my counsel is but half-a-croon,
However, i' th' first place, ye ken the Witch Wallie,
  That bonnie clear spring at the end o' the toon ?

" When the sun frae his bed is beginnin' to teet,
  Gang ye ilka mornin', blaw weet or blaw wind,
And sit by the wallie and dip in your feet,
  Without ere a thocht of the lad in your mind.

" Do this for a week and the cure will be wrocht,
  But, mind ye, tak' care o' what comes in your head ;
If e'er it should chance that the lad be your thocht
  Like the mist o' the mornin' the cantrip will fade."

Thus ended Spunk Janet ; I paid her the fee,
  And by her directions I promised to bide ;
To-morrow the cantrip begins, I maun be
  By the first peep o' day at the Witch Wallie's side.

The cauld o' the water I weel may endure ;
  But then there's the thocht, it's the warst o' it a' ;
For if ower the thochts o' my mind I had pow'r,
  I wadna hae needed Spunk Janet ava.

                                        Robin.

NOTE.—" Spunk Janet " is long since dead. She was
one of the race now almost extinct in Scotland. Janet's
last customer was a servant maid, who, after crawling up
her narrow stair, found Janet seated in an old armchair
with a short " black cutty " in her mouth. " Janet," said
she, " I want my fortune." Alas ! Janet gave no answer.
The gloomy chamber was only tenanted by the old withered
remains of the sorceress. Her spirit had fled, and her fortune
was told.—S.S.

The following poem of Mr. Foozle's is a parody of a poem
which appeared originally in a local volume, written by a
" Young " man. I present it to the reader as found in the
manuscripts of the author.—S.S.

A NEW POEM
on the
Martyrs who suffered death by fire, at St. Andrews,
inter stanzed with

A NEW POEM
on the
Martyrs who suffered at tripe Betts feast,
St. Mary's Close, Dundee.

Y.—Here stand the relics of a former age,
   Where Popish priesthood long did wage ;
   The time worn ruin, and the mouldering tower,
   Licentious rival with unbounded power.

F.—Here stand the relics of a gorge-ous meeting,
   Where Tom and Tindal had a match at eating,
   The load crust worn, and the mouldering scone,
   Licentious rival with a well picked bone.

Y.—Where Beaton sat in crime of pride arrayed,
   Looked on the fire and faggot undismayed,
   And saw the virtuous Wishart meet his fate,
   And smiled to see him in that awful state.

F.—Where Tindal sat in corduroy arrayed,
   Looked on the big fat haggis undismayed,
   And saw voracious Tom urged on by fate,
   Seize on the whole and clap it on his plate.

Y.—I think I see that martyr's humble face
   To heaven uplifted with a holy grace,
   It heavenward bound, in singleness of heart
   For his loved Saviour's sake he felt no dart.

F.—I think I see Tindal's full moon face,
   With paws uplifted as he mumbled grace,
   And then haggisward began to play his part,
   Grasp knife and fork, and at it made a dart.

Y.—The fire is kindled, but that good man's prayer
   (Methinks I hear his voice far, far above the air)
   Sweetly and calm ascends to heaven the while,
   Far, far above the crackling of the burning pile.

F.—The fire is kindled—Bett's busy—she prepares
   (Methinks I hear her voice far, far down the stairs)
   Sweetly the odours up ascends to us the while,
   From a huge wame of tripe upon the red hot pile.

Y.—The fire ascends.   I see his face no more—
　　His pangs have ceased, his troubles now are o'er
　　But God has sanctified his latest breath,
　　And all his earthly woes are closed in death.

F.—Bett's now come up.   Tindal sees her face once more.
　　The tripe is boiled—her troubles now are o'er ;
　　O' tripe ! I'll praise thee with my latest breath ;
　　Before Tom gets a bit I'll suffer death.

Y.—Where are his ashes flown ? No marble tells ;
　　The martyr in a blessed mansion dwells ;
　　To such as him a tomb were needless given,
　　His God remembers him—his tomb is heaven.

F.—Where has the haggis gone ? Tom's belching tells
　　That bag and all within his stomach dwells.
　　Had I ate such my belly must have riven,
　　For ne'er to me was such a stomach given.

Y.—But Beaton met a darker deeper fate—
　　His pomp is ended and his gorgeous state—
　　Doomed to be murdered at a lonely hour,
　　With all the luxury of a lawless power.

F.—But the cow-heel met a dismal, darker fate,
　　'Twas smuggled in Tom's hat, clapt on his " pate,"
　　Doomed to be swallowed at a fitting hour,
　　With all the fury of a bull-dog power.

Y.—The mitred priest, the subtile monks are gone,
　　The abbey's ruined grandeur stands alone ;
　　Here Popish tyranny no more prevails,
　　The bleak wind whistles through the empty aisles.

F.—Old Tindal's floored, big Lazarus* now is gone,
　　Tom as a lofty champion's left alone ;
　　No feat of eating longer here prevails,
　　And Bett had nothing left but empty pails.

Y.—With a low howl, whose melancholy tone,
　　Of all the long past glories now for ever gone,
　　Wakens to our remembrance of those days gone by,
　　Reminding us, that we, like them must die.

* The slang name of an unshapely piece of mortality that was living in
Dundee about forty years ago.   He was connected with the press-gang,
but is long since " dead and rotten."

F.—It makes Tom howl, with a melancholy tone,
    To think his rivals are now for ever gone,
    Waking to his remembrance those days gone by,
    That drunken cronies must like Lazarus die.

Y.—But here has learning reared a splendid dome,
    Where Britain's sons may find a genial home ;
    And pure religion raised her hallowed shrine ;
    And Professors skilled to form the young divine.

F.—Now here . . . Has reared a pretty dome,
    Where ox-tail eaters find a kindred home ;
    And pure brown soup is made for those who dine,
    With puddings, pies, and good Madeira wine.

Y.—Thou ancient city, blessed be thy name,
    And like the Rock of Ages be thy fame,
    Thy sons and daughters good and pure,
    May in St. Andrew's record still endure.*

F.—Thou ancient Betty, blessed be thy name,
    In St. Mary's close, high bronzed up be thy fame ;
    Thy sons and only daughter good and pure,
    May they in thy " tripe temple," still endure.

Y.—May a poet's blessings ever rest on thee,
    And thy good people, may they still be free :
    Accept this poem, I humbly do implore,
    And may heaven bless you and yours for evermore.

F.—Accept this poem, Bett, it will this story tell,
    That our martyrs were dead-drunk before they fell
    At " Tumble Down's " they've both " run up a score,"
    Which, if you'll pay, they'll praise you evermore.

* I do not wonder at Mr. Foozle ridiculing this incomprehensible blether.—S.S.
  The whole of the persons mentioned in this parody were associates of Mr. Foozle's : " Tom and Tindal," are fictitious names given to two well-known characters in Dundee.—S.S.

The Twa Phantoms

Wild, dark, and dismal was the nicht,
    Down on the streets the rain was plashin',
And aye again wild gusts o' wind
    Wad send the slates and lum-heads crashin'.

THE "NEW"

Palais de Danse

*(Managed and Personally Supervised by
Mr. and Mrs. Jas. Duncan)*

SOUTH TAY STREET, DUNDEE

❧

Dancing   Nightly

and

Wednesday and Saturday Afternoons

❧

Private   Dances

Are Exclusively Booked

SUCCESS ASSURED!

Phone 5020.

Wi' distant murr ilk gust began—
  Gust met wi' gust in swirlin' bustle—
Now rising in a fiendish howl,
  Then deeing awa in sickly whustle.

The tempest summon'd a' its micht
  When wearing near the hour of twel'.
And frae its wildest, highest heicht,
  At ance down to a whisper fell.

Its rage was ower. The Cowgate bell
  The langest hour melodious rang ;
The Steeple could the same tale tell,
  But tauld it wi' a heavier clang.

When a' the bells had ceased to ring,
  And folk had turn'd them round to sleep,
The mune, like some enchanted thing,
  Frae 'tween the clouds began to peep.

Now sic a chance ! An instant, and
  The wildest blast that e'er was blawn—
That ever harried sea or land—
  Has down to deadly silence faun.

The draps that frae the house-heads fa',—
  The watchman's tramp we now could hear ;
A brichter mune ne'er shone abune.
  'Twas temptin' to gang out to see 'er.

Sae frae my cozie bed I rose,
  And wandered out the mune to see ;
Lord, how she glower'd, and, what was strange
  She shone on nae place but Dundee !

I had a great desire to mark
  The mysteries o' this wondrous nicht,
And dandered up by Dudhope Park
  To try and get a better sicht.

Queer was the nicht. Far in the east,
  Whereon my een could hardly gaze.
A flaming fire cam' frae the sea—
  'Twas Luckie-Scaup a' in a blaze.

North-west, and near by Camperdown,
  But high abune it in the air,
There hung a bluish white-like cloud,
  Wherefrae there stream'd a silvery glare.

And on Balgay a phantom stood,
  Anither ane on the Law ;
Each in its hand a trumpet had
  And time aboot did blaw.

And then low down on Logie Kirkyaird
  I chanced to turn my een ;
That something was transactin' there,
  Was plainly to be seen.

Ilk phantom as it blaw'd its blast,
  To gie the loudest strave ;
At ilka blast, by Logie Kirk,
  There open'd up a grave.

At ilka blast that frae the Law
  Cam' wi' rebounding rair,
A form rose frae out the grave,
  And mounted in the air.

Mounting in the air it gaed,
  Until it did alicht
Upo' the bonnie blue-white cloud,
  That shone sae fair and bricht.

As soon as it had lichted there,
  The cloud broke through in twain ;
And as the form enter'd in
  It closed up again.

Nae sooner had the cloud been closed,
  Than frae it gliding cam
A slow, harmonious, hauly strain,
  Like the " Auld Hundred Psalm."

At ilka blast the phantom gave
  That stood upon Balgay,
The form that rose frae the grave
  Gaed bleezin' down the Tay.

Unto a tattery bunch o' fire
  To turn the form seem'd ;
And as it hurried down the Tay
  The waters bizz'd and steam'd.

And when it came to Luckie-Scaup
  Down in the fire it fell ;
Blue fuming flames cam' spewin' up,
  And brocht a sulphury smell.

And what a clang o' tongues and chains
    Cam volleying up the firth,
Seeming to come up wi' the flames
    Frae the inside o' the earth.

Then did the phantom on Balgay
    Upon a whustle blaw,
And a' was silence down below—
    Ye'd heard a preen head fa'.

When a' the graves were open'd out
    Ilk phantom took its flicht ;
The ane ascended frae the Law,
    And on the cloud did licht ;
Then did it gie its henmost blaw
    And vanish out o' sicht.

The ane that stood upon Balgay
    Assum'd another form ;
The fire that darted frae his een
    Micht tell a coming storm.

The Tay was now like ocean wild,
    High mounting to the skies !
Now springs the phantom off Balgay—
    Now on a wave he lies.

His wave is now on fire. See how
    To Luckie-Scaup it swells.
Again begins the clang o' chains ;
    Again the fiendish yells.

Now frae his mou', now frae his nose,
    The burning brimstane fumes !
Now is his trumpet gone and he
    A fiery fork assumes.

That some queer trick he'd yet to play
    Was weel seen by the cant o'm ;
But here the sun laup frae the sea
    And put to fricht the phantom.

   .   .   .   .

Black nicht went hirpling o'er the hills,
    And witchery with it went,
Leaving no trace behind ; the grass
    Was all with dew besprent,
And the virtuous morn found the earth
    All green and innocent.

I wander'd hame richt sair amazed,
    At what I'd heard and seen ;
My head was turn'd as nearly craz'd
    As ever head has been :
To see dead men and women rais'd
    Is a fearsome thing I ween.

Were I to tell you what it meant
    You'd curse me o'er and o'er ;
Nor would your sleep be so sound and deep
    As it has been before.
This I may say—THERE WILL BE A DAY
    WHEN ALL OF US—YOU, I, AND THEY
THAT HAVE BEEN, AND—but away ! away !
    I may not tell you more.

An Eccentric Dundee Barber's visit to Michael Faraday

Amongst many other interesting matters that he has left
recorded, the later Alexander Maxwell (the author of *The
History of Old Dundee*, and for several years a Magistrate of
the Burgh), gives the following account of a conversation
he had with an eccentric Barber, George Boyd, who throws
rather an interesting light on the early life of Michael Faraday.
George was over eighty years of age, and a notable propagator
of news and gossip. " He was very deaf," writes Mr. Maxwell,
" and heard nothing except what filtered through his ear
trumpet, so that when he wanted to silence an interlocutor
and have all the talk, he had simply to hold it down." This
plan he had probably adopted in his conversation with Mr.
Maxwell, for what follows is evidently all on George's side.
The subject under discussion had been the lectures of the
Watt Institution, to which Mr. Maxwell was secretary.
" Eh ! Is he a lecturer at the Watt Institution ? Ye get mony
wise men to lecture there. I ken a curious lecturing man
up in London. Faraday they ca' him—Michael Faraday.
He lectures at the Royal Institootion. Her Majesty peys
him weel for 't, an' he has a gey guid job. Jamie Faraday,
his father, was a smith, an' at ae time wis oot o' wark, an'
sair put to in manteening his wife an' twa or three laddies.
So he gaed up to England seekin' wark, an' my brither
ga'e him a job. When he fand him steady an' weel-behaved
he made him foreman, an' he wis lang wi' him. Michael
was the auldest o' the family, an' his mither no' being very

stout he used to work at hame just like a lassie at onything he could dae to help her, an' wis aye a biddable laddie. He had an awfu' notion of books, an' used to sit up at nicht efter the lave were in their beds readin' an' studyin' by himsel'. He was aye plouterin' wi' water o' different colours, an' sometimes brakin' his mither's dishes makin' what he ca'ed expeeriments, an' wad gar curious mixtures fizzle an' gae aff wi' great pluffs till the very cat got fleggit an' ran awa'. But for a' that, Michael wes aye a cautious, weel-doin' laddie, an' had mony freens. Weel, efter he wes groun up, Humphrey Davy, him that ye'll maybe hae heard o', wha learned fowk a' the wit o' the warld, took him for a 'prentice at the Royal Institootion, where he's aye been sin-syne, for after Humphrey dee'd he got his place.

"Weel, ye see, I was up in London shortly syne seein' my laddie. It's a place I never likit', for I wes aye daved an' dumfonn'ered wi' th' din o' coaches blatterin' up an' doon th' causey ; but I wes unco happy wi' my ain fowk. I used to see the professor, as they ca' him, gey aften at the meetin' on Sabbaths an' he wes aye wantin' me to gae an' get tea wi' him an' the mistress. But I said—' na, na, Faraday ! I winna dae that, for I wad loss mysel' on thae streets o' yours.' But ae day he cam' to me when the meetin' wes skellin', an' he says—' I'll tak' ye to your tea the nicht, Geordie.' So wi' that he brocht in bye a coach an' put me in, then cam' in himsel', an' shuttin' the door, tell't the coachman to drive to the Royal Institootion. ' Eh ! Faraday, but ye hae me noo.' The coachman kent the road brawly, and brocht us up to the very door. Eh, but it was a great big hoose, wi' pillars an muckle staps along the foreside, an' windows a' roond about. Weel, when we got in, we had four hours hearty. Forbye me an' my laddie, he had two or three o' his professors, wha were as denty chaps as ever ye saw, an' I wes juist at hame wi' them. Efter we had crackit' a while, I says, ' Man, Faraday, this is a braw hoose ye hae, but I wad like to ken what ye dae. What is't ye work at ? ' ' Weel, Geordie,' he says, ' come an' I'll let ye see what I dae.' So he took me up a stair an' roond a lang passage to a little door, an openin' it he says. ' This is where I work, Geordie.' When I gaed in I saw it was a big place seated just like a kirk, wi' tables that had mony strange wheelmaleeries, an' on the wa's there were bottles filled wi' curious stuff like what Davie Greig hes roond his shop. ' Ye're a queer chield, Faraday ! Ye're a queer chield ! Ay, man, is that ye'r gibbals ? But what dae ye do wi' them ? I wad like to ken that.' ' I'll let you see,' says he. Wi' that he just touched twa wires thegither, and the gas lighted up at the ither end o' the place. Syne he garred set a basin o' water on the table, and takin' a sma bottle frae the shelf, he poured in a little red stuff, an' wi' that the water gaed a-fire, an' burned wi' a green lowe. So I got feared an' said : ' Ye're no' canny, Faraday ! ye're no' canny ! For ither fowk licht their gas wi' lucifer matches, but I think, yours is lichtit be Lucifer himsel', an' water pets oot a common fire, but your fire burns the water up. I'll awa' doon to the mistress an' see if her bottles ha'e onything better in them nor yours.' " " Professor Faraday," Mr. Maxwell concludes, " while one of our foremost men of science, at whose feet Princes loved to sit, was of a very modest and unobtrusive disposition, and seemed to fee that he occupied his highest place when opening up the words of Scripture to a humble congregation of Glasites. When he came on a visit to Dundee, he loved to meet with those belonging to that body there. I hoped to have got him to lecture at the Watt Institution, but his time would not permit of it."

Michael Faraday was born in 1791, and began life as an apprentice to a London bookbinder. He became an assistant to Sir Humphrey Davy, and was made Professor of Chemistry in the Royal Institution in 1833. He was the greatest experimental chemist of his age. He died in 1867. Sir Humphrey Davy was once asked, " What do you consider your greatest discovery ? " He at once replied—" Michael Faraday."

Jenny Marshall's Candy, O

Tune.—" I'm ower young to marry yet."

Chorus.—O, Jenny Marshall, Jenny Marshall,
     Jenny Marshall's candy, O ;
  I always like to patronise
     Jenny Marshall's candy, O.
  When going along the Nethergate,
     There's nought can be so handy, O,
  As dropping in to get a stick
     Of Jenny Marshall's candy, O.

Ye'll get a stick as streicht's a rash,
   A crookit ane, or bandy, O ;
The grandest treat, for little cash,
   Is Jenny Marshall's candy O.
The ladies fine come in the street,
   Wi' dresses a' fu' dandy, O ;
And weel like their mou's to weet
   Wi' Jenny Marshall's candy, O.
There's no lass in a' Dundee,
   Frae modest dame to randy, O,
But wha wad want her cup o' tea
   For Jenny Marshall's candy, O.
There's no a loon in a' the town,
   A Jamie, Jock, or Sandy, O,
But wha wad want his piece at noon
   For Jenny Marshall's candy, O.
When weety winter wi' the hoast,
   Is like to rive and rend ye, O ;
The best o' cures at little cost,
   Is Jenny Marshall's candy, O.
Some uses draps o' peppermint,
   To kill the smell o' brandy, O ;
But, by my shuith I'm weel content
   Wi' Jenny Marshall's Candy, O.
Then come awa', baith great an' sma',
   And lat your purse attend ye, O,
And, while ye find a baubee in't,
   Buy Jenny Marshall's Candy, O.

                      ROBERT LEIGHTON.

Jenny Marshall's shop was situated in the Nethergate near where St. Paul's Church now stands. It was a famous resort of lads and lasses on the summer evenings, when Jenny drove a roaring trade. The song was sung by " Blind Hughie " on the streets, and became very popular. Jenny was very much annoyed about it, and consulted a lawyer if she could not get " that loon Bob Leighton punished for his impudence."

Question and Answer

One of our civic functionaries, whose jolly appearance gives ample indication of excellent " keep," happened lately to be enjoying the cool air on the beautiful promenade at the Barracks, no doubt ruminating on the share he had in the management of the bustling world below. In his ramble to the westward, he came up to the sentinel at the powder magazine. " Well," said he, " my good friend, can I get out by the west gate ? " The sentinel, disposing of the question in a literal sense, replied—" I do not know, sir ; but a cart-load of hay came through it this afternoon."

The Mylnefield Mob

Saunders Logan, of noted memory, before proceeding to the scene of conflict, very kindly gave his advice to his wife and children. " First Jock an' Meg. You, Jock Logan, protect yer mither, for your father is gaen to ficht wi' the mighty ; and you, Meg, be a dutifu' bairn to yer mither when Saunders is awa', an' his head happit." The turkey-cock at this moment uttered a terrible scream, on which the heroic Saunders roared out to his wife, " Protect yersel Jean, for I maun rin."

Saunders Again

Saunders, on one occasion, starved himself for nearly a week, that he might get a real gutsfu' at an approaching christening. On the morning of the auspicious day, a waggish neighbour looked in, and told Saunders that the " affair " had been postponed, advising him, at the same time, to relieve the necessities of his stomach with a plentiful supply of brose. Saunders accordingly did so before discovering the hoax, and thus rendered himself utterly unable to get more than a mere taste of the dainties.

A Predicament

One day a slater, employed on the roof of a house in the Overgate, lost his hold, and was slowly descending to apparently inevitable destruction—repeating to himself all the time— " O, sic a fa's I will get ! O' sic a fa's I will get ! " He certainly did fall to the ground, but was fortunately little injured. A man, not aware of the " dooncome," happened to pass ere the poor fellow had well recovered his senses, and asked if he knew what o'clock it was ? " No," replied the slater ; " but I guess it's aboot denner-time, for I saw the folks busy suppin' their kail i' the garret as I cam doon the slates ! "

Town Officers—" Couter Mackay."

The Magistrates and Council walked in procession every Sunday to the Old or East Church, the east or royal gallery of which was set apart for their use, where the town officers and their halberts were also accommodated. Although the inhabitants were a quiet and douce set of folks, the authorities had sometimes to avail themselves of the services of the burgh officers in preserving the peace, particularly among the rising generation of youths, who appeared to enjoy frequently the practice of quarrelling and having a fight or " trap "—*i.e.*, the boys inhabiting one district of the town throwing stones at one another till a victory was secured by making the enemy take to their heels. Sometimes the sagacious town officers made an unexpected appearance and apprehended a few of the combatants, placing them in durance vile in a cellar below the Town House named " the thief's hole," where, after being kept in the dark for an hour or two, they were relieved with an admonition. One of the officials was named William Mackay, an old private in the grenadier company of a Highland regiment, and his Celtic admonitions were so very expressive that all the boys looked upon him as a veritable " terror to evildoers." His height was about six feet, and, like the Duke of Wellington, he possessed such a prominence of nasal organ as to be best known by the name of " Couter Mackay."

One Sunday forenoon, when the congregation in the East Church were assembled, and the Rev. Dr. Davidson was engaged in conducting the services, a sparrow found its way into the church, the upper windows being open for ventilation in consequence of the heat of the summer weather. The whole attention of the worshippers was attracted to the gyrations of the little bird, which, after flying back and fore along the length of the church, perched itself on the pinnacle above the canopy of the pulpit, and leisurely surveyed the attentive faces of the congregation. Apparently desirous of again exercising its wings, the " wee bird," after fluttering along the ceiling, perched itself upon the peak of the back of the Provost's chair, when William Mackay, thinking, like a good old soldier, that an act of insubordination was thereby committed in the bird presuming to perch itself higher than his commanding officer (the Provost), stepped from his pew in the back of the gallery with the view of compelling the

28 Hunter Street, DUNDEE.

Phone 3525.

***

David Brown, M.B.I.E.

Funeral Director.   Certificated Embalmer.

Cremations arranged.

***

266 Hilltown, DUNDEE.

Phone 2734.

DAVID WHAMOND

Specialist in
HIGH-CLASS
GROCERIES,
PROVISIONS,
WINES AND
SPIRITS

Our Motto—
SATISFIED
CUSTOMERS

TOP   OF   HILLTOWN,   DUNDEE

PHONE 3370.

birdie to relinquish its position. Whether William's *proboscis* frightened the bird, or whether it resolved to allow the congregation to resume attention to the words of the preacher, it is not easy to decide ; but on seeing the Town Guardsman approach the municipal pew, it flew away with a scream out of the open window by which it had entered the church, when the countenances of the congregation resumed their usual quiet and devout expression.

William's sagacity was again displayed at the time of the election of Councillors under the new sett of the burgh, prescribed by the Court of Session after the town's disfranchisement in 1828. It had been the practice of the self-elected Council under the old close burgh system to have an occasional glass of toddy together in the Town Hall, the liquor being mixed in a large Indian china bowl, which had been presented to the Council some time about the end of last century. On the occasion of the first meeting under the Provostship of Mr. Robert Jobson (commonly called Riga Rob), it was observed that the celebrated punch-bowl had disappeared from its place in the hall. The Provost made inquiry on the subject, and found that William Mackay had sagaciously concluded that the old Magistrates, with their cocked hats and silk gowns, having been dismissed by the electors, and a new reforming economical Council elected in their stead, the best thing he could do was to put the bowl out of sight as an unbecoming utensil under the new *régime*. But for once William was at fault, for the Provost ordered the bowl to be placed on the table, and he, his fellow Magistrates, and the members of Council had a jolly glass of the national liquor together, and the bowl now occupies a prominent position in a recess in the south wall immediately behind the Provost's chair.

William had a son named Patrick, a smart man, who was largely employed by the members of the legal profession as a messenger-at-arms, and was considered one of the most active criminal officers of Scotland. At that time the modern system of county and burgh police was not in existence, and Patrick Mackay was often employed in apprehending criminals in this district, in which calling he was considered to excel. Patrick was a gentlemanly fellow, and was on good social terms with the Dundee writers. A friend of his, in good employment in the profession, on purchasing and furnishing a spacious mansion in the west end, invited Patrick to a bachelor dinner ; and, after showing him through the rooms, the lawyer asked

Patrick what he thought of it all. Patrick, who was a sort of a wag, could not resist the temptation to give a jocular answer, and, quietly turning to his entertainer, said, " Weel, David, I think it would make a ' glorious poind.' " This, besides smelling too much of the shop, and being calculated to give offence, was only at the time treated as a good joke with mutual laughter ; but it was noticed by the friends of the parties that Patrick never again enjoyed the honour of an invitation to S——d House.

An Erudite Drummer

Another of the old town officers was named Daniel M'Cormick, who was a man of superior education and a great linguist. About the year 1828, when the writer (J. M. Beatts) of these sketches was attending the Grammar School, Dan used to set himself on the façade wall on the south or Nethergate side of the Town's Churches, and, surrounded by the boys, put questions to them about their studies in the Latin and Greek languages, and kindly helped them out with whatever they expressed a difficulty in mastering. Dan acted as town drummer, and on one occasion he was requested by a Hebrew Professor to give notice to the townsmen of an intended lecture on the Hebrew language. Dan took the liberty of inquiring as to the system upon which he taught that difficult language, showing his knowledge of the various systems of tuition so intimately that the Professor, seeing that the town drummer was such an adept, thought that the Dundonian *savants* would be likely to overwhelm him with their erudition ; so, deeming discretion the better part of valour, he quietly left the town, remarking that surely the inhabitants must be a colony sprung from the lost tribes of Israel.

A Near-sighted Minister

The writer (J. M. Beatts) of these notes in his boyhood attended the Old or East Church, he and his fellow-scholars being accommodated with sittings in the west gallery, belonging to the town. The internal arrangements were very different from those in the present building, erected in the place of the old one after its destruction by fire. The pulpit was placed against one of the large stone pillars supporting the arches of the interior wall. The lateran was carried from one side of the pulpit round the back of the pillar to the other side, forming a semi-circle. One Sunday a larger number of parents and infants for baptism than usual occupied the whole space round, and the officiating preacher (the Rev. Dr. Davidson), after concluding his sermon, turned to the lateran and desired the parents to present their children. Two of the parents nearest the pulpit held up their respective children, which order was also obeyed by those not in sight of the minister. After the two were duly admitted to the membership of the Christian Church by the sprinkling of water, the Doctor, who was short-sighted and wore spectacles, turned round to the congregation and commenced prayer. Before, however, he had repeated many of the words, the parties occupying the muncipal gallery appeared suddenly to display considerable suppressed risibility in their countenances, when Provost Bell called out from his position in the centre seat in the front of the gallery, " Dr. Davidson, you have omitted to baptise some children " ; the Doctor at once stopped, turned to the side of his pulpit, where other parents had placed themselves on those retiring who had already received the benefit of the ordinance, and the sprinkling was continued till no more candidates made their appearance. The Doctor then quietly resumed where he had left off, and the services were closed as usual.

One of the " Unco Guid "

About the first decade of last century a rather flourishing trade was carried on in Greenland whale fishing. in which not only the shipowners but also the seafaring population took a deep interest. When the ships left the harbour, which most of them did on the same day, the shore was crowded with friends and well-wishers, male and female, and the departures were marked by three cheers from the respective crews, responded to by three cheers from the crowds at the harbour. In the fall of the year considerable anxiety was generally felt by all interested to learn as soon as possible the result of the exertions of the different crews and calculations made by the sailors' wives as to the amount of oil money their husbands may have earned. A principal owner of one of the ships was a successful merchant and very pious pillar of the Kirk, who resided in a mansion situated at the south side of the Nethergate. This gentleman had in his employment a man named John Duncan, who took care of the counting-house at the shore, ran messages

E

and made himself generally useful.   In the fall of a certain
year the rest of the whale ships had arrived, but there were
for some time no tidings of the vessel belonging to John's
master, and he was several times sent to the party acting as
manager, or " ship's husband," as the term was then used,
inquiring whether any tidings had been heard of the missing
vessel, but without effect.

Early on a Sunday morning the vessel made her appearance
in the river, and it occurred to John that the best thing he
could do was to go and tell his master, and accordingly he
set off to the Nethergate, and on being admitted by the maid,
desired her to say that he wished particularly to see him.
The maid said that master and the family were engaged at
breakfast, and if John would wait till that was over he would
likely be admitted to an audience ; but John could not agree
to this ; he must see him at once, and could not wait, as he
had to go home for his wife, who had arranged to accompany
him to the Tabernacle (now St. David's Established Church)
to hear the great preacher, Mr. Haldane.   On this being
stated to the master orders were issued for John being
admitted at once.   John took off his hat, walked into the
room, and to the astonishment, and probably to the satisfaction
of the family assembled, blurted out, " Mr. T., the Greenland
has come in, and is anchored in the roads."   The master,
instead of thanking John for the news, rose from his chair,
and expressed his surprise that John should so far forget
himself as to come with any news about business to him on
the Lord's Day, and told his crestfallen employee to suspend
any further intelligence on the subject till to-morrow, and
accompanied John from the room into the lobby for the
purpose of showing him out of the house.   Before leaving
him to find his way out, however, the master came up to
John's side, placed his mouth in close proximity to John's
ear, and in an audible whisper said, " John, my man, did you
hear if she was weel fished ? "   John, being a little nettled at
his reception, turned his head, and looking in his master's
face, intimated that he would act upon his master's godly
advice, and tell him the particulars " the morn."

A Dundee Roscius

Early last century the Theatre Royal, Castle Street,
had for a lessee a Scotsman named Corbet Ryder, a
jolly, goodhearted, gentlemanly man.   At that time, the

inhabitants numbering only about 35,000, the patronage of the small theatre-going portion of the population was found insufficient to meet the necessary expenditure, and therefore, Mr. Ryder was sometimes favoured by the services of distinguished local amateurs, so as to secure a house. Among those amateurs was a young man named Peter Pullar, the son of a respected member of the baker trade, who had a strong inclination to adopt the *rôle* of a tragedian, and who made overtures to the theatrical manager with a view to acting on a certain night the character of Richard III. His services were thankfully accepted, although some who knew Peter feared that his natural impetuosity and eccentricity would, in the character of a royal despot, lead to something out of the common. On the night appointed the house, to the agreeable surprise of the struggling lessee, was a complete bumper. When Peter appeared he was received with a perfect ovation by boxes, pit, and gallery, and during the early scenes he managed to *wamble* through the part with some degree of credit. When the play progressed to the tent scene, in which it is understood that the king is wakened out of his sleep, in which he dreamed that he was in the midst of a fight for his blood-stained throne, Peter appeared much excited, and looked " to the manner born " as if he were actually the bloodthirsty Glo'ster whom he was permitted to represent on the stage. Sword in hand he advanced towards the footlights, calling out—

" A horse, a horse, my kingdom for a horse ! "

Now, at that time there was no Gas Company in existence in Dundee. Whale oil formed the combustible element of illumination, and the footlights consisted of what was called Argand lamps, each having a reservoir containing a sufficient supply of oil to last for the evening. In uttering the cry regarding the needful quadruped, Peter seemed disappointed that nothing like a specimen of the equine breed answered to his call, and immediately, grasping more tightly his royal sword, he brought the blade with a swing along the row of footlights, smashing the glasses to atoms, bursting the reservoirs of oil and scattering the same right and left among the ladies and gentlemen in the adjacent boxes, and inundating the music books and instruments of the orchestra with the treasures of the Arctic ocean. This brought affairs to a climax. The boxes moaned, the pit grinned, and the gallery cheered the redoubtable stage-struck hero till the rafters rang. This incident caused great stir in the town, and a well-executed engraving of the attack on the footlights was published, showing a striking likeness of Peter in his royal robes in the act of smashing the footlights. Peter was not afforded another opportunity of strutting upon the stage in his native town.

A Change of Occupation

A Mr. Bass, a born tragedian, who was sometime after lessee of the Theatre had in his employment two actors named Power and Croley, who were very popular as actors, but who had commenced business in Bolton as butchers. A theatre-going friend asked Mr. Bass what had become of the of the two good actors, when Mr. B. raised his right hand, and placing himself in a theatrical position somewhat similar to that in which Ajax is generally represented in *tableaux vivant* answered, " Power and Croley have changed their swords into butchers' knives."

English Tam

In the first quarter of last century an Englishman named Tomlinson came to Dundee and opened a butcher's shop at the corner of Hilltown and Bucklemaker Wynd. From the lowest degree of impecuniosity he succeeded in arriving at a very remunerative trade, and although he did not advertise in the grandiloquent style now popular, he was known to give good bargains of butcher meat. When children came to buy he gave a much greater bargain to them than he would have done had the head of the family come to make the purchase. Tom liked to encourage the rising generation whose parents had a struggle for existence, and there are still alive (1883) some who in adverse times were sent to Tom's shop to buy a bone to make soup for the family, who otherwise would not then have been blessed with the smell of butcher meat. Tom when in his cups was wont to give a lucid description of his entrance into business. He confessed that he had only a few shillings of capital, and with this money he managed to purchase a large old boar, which he killed and dressed to the best advantage, and with which he was enabled to meet the demands of customers whether they wanted beef, mutton, veal, or pork, the cuts being so well-assorted that it would have puzzled a Philadelphian lawyer to know that " Sandy Campbell's " hide had enclosed such a variety of butcher meats. Tom was a bit of a Bluebeard, and did not scruple at administering punishment to his help-mate by locking her in the killing-house, which was situated at the back of the shop. He had a son, a tall, strong giant, who was implicated in the " sack " of the Police Office in 1831, for which offence he was sentenced by the Justiciary Court in Edinburgh to a term of imprisonment.

Cossack Jock

About the year 1813 a man resided in Dundee who was known by the name of " Cossack Jock "—a harmless individual, a little light in the upper storey, and a military enthusiast. He succeeded in gathering around him an awkward squad of young lads, taught them the goose step, and drilled them into the marching and manual exercises. These, sometimes to the number of 40 or 50, marched through the town, led by a band composed of about half a dozen, playing on penny whistles and old pans turned upside down, which served for drums. This demonstration generally took place when the mail coach arriving in Dundee brought newspapers narrating a successful effort by the British army under Welling-ton in its ultimately successful attempt to drive the French armies out of the Spanish peninsula. Jock was rather a favourite with the citizens, and latterly a number of the inhabitants resolved to afford him the means of earning a livelihood by industry. They accordingly raised a subscription for the purpose of presenting him with a pleasure boat, so that it might be let out to parties wishing a sail on the river. A very handsome boat was procured, and Jock selected a crew to navigate it from the ranks of his volunteer company. On a Sunday morning Jock engaged with a party of about a dozen males and females to give them a sail on the river. After cruising about for some time the boat was by a sudden squall capsized about the middle of the river, and Jock, his crew, and the whole of the passengers were drowned. This melancholy occurrence created a great sensation in the town, and the news having been communicated to the people assembled in the churches the preachers were in a few minutes left with only a few of their hearers. The occasion was " improved " by the Sabbatarians as a just judgment on those

William Mackenzie

(William M. MacLean, Sole Proprietor)

30, North Lindsay Street,

TELEPHONE
3081
(20 lines)

Dundee

TELEGRAMS
"CERTAIN"
DUNDEE

TURF AND FOOTBALL COMMISSION AGENT

Place your bets with the well-known local man and get the BEST TERMS obtainable anywhere

FOOTBALL

Nothing ever barred, and better prices than others

The oldest established Agent north of the Forth

Established since 1909

guilty of the sin of Sabbath-breaking, denunciations to that effect being launched from the pulpits by some of the ministers of the Gospel in language which nowadays would be considered the extreme of Christian intolerance.

A Right-of-way Heroine

In the early part of the last century there lived in Dundee an elderly lady of rather eccentric habits.   She was connected with respectable families, but lived solitary, with only one servant.   She had a peculiar taste in dress, and liked to be noticed by the respectable portion of the inhabitants.   Being possessed of property and means, she had both the power and the will to exhibit her independence of spirit, and in consequence of what the populace considered her aristocratic manners   she   went   under   the   designation   of   "Madame Geekie."   The old public Meadows originally consisted of three pieces of meadow land belonging to different individuals. The town was possessed of a small meadow adjoining, and the other meadows belonged to William Kinloch, Andrew Barrie, and John Lovel.   Between these there originally ran a road connecting   the   town   with   the   Chapelshade.   When   the whole of these meadows fell into the hands of the burgh authorities, and all except Andrew Barrie's were surrounded by a stone wall, the old road was still kept open, although gates were placed at each end, so as to be closed at night, especially on the nights set apart for watching the green and thus protecting the clothes laid out for bleaching by the inhabitants.   These gates were regularly kept open, however, during the daytime ; but in the course of time the town officers either by order of their superiors or of their own motive, began to be rather indifferent about keeping open the thoroughfare, and some days they did not open them at all, so that those requiring to go from town to the Chapelshade, or vice versa, had to go round by the Dudhope Road on the west, or by the Tod's Burn Road on the east, of the Meadows. What is everybody's business as usual was nobody's business, although the complaints were loud and deep.   But Nemesis appeared in the shape of "Madame Geekie," who boldly bearded Provost Riddoch for the illegal attempt to encroach on the public rights.   Her effort was successful, and with a written order to the officer of the day she presented herself at the guardhouse and demanded access to the meadow thoroughfare. On receiving the document William Mackay, the orderly for the week, at once complied with the request, and Madame, in presence of a large number of the lieges, male and female, in dignified triumph walked along the whole way to the Chapelshade amid the cheers and loudly expressed good wishes of her admiring townspeople.

A Plucky Barber

In the beginning of last century there lived in Dundee several eccentric characters in humble life whose escapades formed sources of amusement to the inhabitants when little novelty in the way of entertainment or amusement was afforded, the town being in a way shut up from all intercourse with the rest of the world from want of the locomotion which is now so abundantly provided. Near the top of Couttie's Wynd, Nethergate, was located a barber named John Murray, a sort of half-witted, impulsive character, who used to narrate his juvenile adventures to his customers. It was the practice on Saturday afternoons for the doors of the Old Steeple to be opened for the admission of the public at a small charge, and the schoolboys used to avail themselves of the opportunity to run up the stairs, count the 365 steps, and land at the second bartizan, whence is obtained an extensive panoramic view of the surrounding country, the river, and the North Sea. Johnny Murray and some of his schoolfellows were one day chasing each other round the bartizan when a sparrow was espied entering a hole in the outside wall below the cornice with a bit of bread in its beak. It was at once concluded that a nest with young ones was inside, and it was resolved to try to get access to the nest ; but the aperture being some distance below, it was difficult to get any boy willing to " bell the cat " and harry the nest. Johnny proposed that he would go outside, provided one of the boys would hold on at one side of his Highland bonnet while he suspended himself by the other. This plan was at last adopted, and as Johnny swung himself over at a height of about 130 feet he addressed the boy who had hold of the bonnet very solemnly in these words (Johnny had a halt in his speech)— " Giff you dinna h-h-haud the gr-gr-grips you'll no' get nane o' the sp-spurdies." After which adjuration he carefully handed up the young fledglings to his companions and returned to a position of safety.

Bridie Andrew

In the first quarter of last century a man who went under the above popular appellation might be heard every night with shrill voice calling out " Hot Pies " as he plodded along the streets. As he arrived at the door of a public-house or brewer's alehouse he would put his head into the doorway and call out " Any warm pies there." This man and his calling were so familiar that everyone knew and respected him. The above name was not his real patronymic. Andrew Bathie was his real name, and " Bridie " the name which the Forfar people give to their peculiar shaped pies. supposed to have been preferred by the denizens of Dundee. Andrew was a great favourite, especially among the seafaring portion of the population. The peculiarity of this man was his possession of a shrill, powerful voice, which in a quiet evening was heard at the other side of the river Tay. The following incident narrated here, and authorised by his son. who is still ali.·e (1883), will show the kindly good humour with which Andrew was met by those with whom he came in contact. Having a son in London, he had frequently expressed his desire to visit him and get a sight of London, and at that time the only practical mode of conveyance between Dundee and that city was by the smacks belonging to the Dundee, Perth, and London Shipping Company. To enable Andrew to obtain his wish, a number of the shipmasters agreed to procure a passage for him to London and back on condition that, on entering the Thames, Andrew should, when nearing any vessel, give his usual cry of " hot pies." This agreement was faithfully carried out, and it is said that many Dundee sailors scattered among the ships belonging to other than their native ports. on hearing the well-known cry, got upon the ratlines of their vessels, and gave three hearty cheers for " Bonnie Dundee " and " Bridie Andrew." Andrew latterly required to use a pair of crutches in consequence of weakness in his legs, but was very fleet in his locomotion, so much so that on a townsman calling him a cripple he at once challenged the offending party to shew his superiority in going over the ground by trying a race between Dundee and Perth any morning he liked. Well, the bet was taken, Andrew's opponent having no doubt that he was bound to win. but he found he had greatly miscalculated. for the crutches gave Andrew.

E*

whose arms and lungs were of the best material, such an advantage that he spanged over the ground and out-distanced his antagonist before he had proceeded half way, and his opponent had no reason but to give in and declare " cripple " Andrew the victor.

The Polite Town Bellman

About forty years ago (1843) the office of town bellman was held by a man named Joseph Dempster, who had been bred to the shoemaking business, but who in his latter days exchanged his *last* for the *bell* of the public crier. Joseph was an admirable bellman, and possessed naturally a sufficiently abundant supply of the *suaviter in modo* for any purpose ; his voice was very flexible and full-toned, and his intonation and gestures in delivering public announcements were quite unique. No courtier or Frenchman could have done it with more grace and polite humour. One day a military officer, located with his regiment in the Dudhope Barracks, called on Joe, and employed him to proclaim the loss of a dog, and a reward to the finder. Joe did so for three days running, when he was informed that the quadruped had been recovered. Joe thought that he had better call on the gallant holder of His Majesty's commission, but after repeated calls he found the same answer, " Not at home." At last he resolved to make a bold push to see his debtor, believing that the excuse was all sham. He accordingly presented himself at the officer's quarters, and as usual desired his servant to intimate that payment of the bellman's fee was required. The servant proceeded to do so, but Joseph, instead of waiting in the lobby, quietly followed the servant to the door of the officer's room, where he overheard him desire his servant to say that he was " not at home." Joseph at once put his head inside the door and said, " May it please your honour to say when you will be at home." His " honour " roughly demanded who he was, and Joseph at once entered the room, and, hat in hand, with the politest of bows, said, " I am the *honourable* the Bellman of Dundee, at your service." The officer enquired what was the amount of his charge. Joseph answered, " Your pleasure, sir " ; on which he enquired if half-a-crown would satisfy. Joseph expressed himself well satisfied with the allowance, and in thanking his employer he ended by saying, " Good morning, sir ! you are a *right honourable* gentleman."

Willie Harrow

In the early part of last century there resided in Dundee three brothers named William, Andrew, and Thomas Taylor, by occupation carters. William, the eldest, was a little weak, but an exceedingly droll character. He had a squint eye, and the muscles of his face assumed various phases and expressions of countenance by a twitching of the nervous system, always either ludicrous or humorous. The whole three had large front teeth in the upper jaw, the two centre ones being some distance from each other, which gave the observer the idea of their being similar to the teeth of a harrow, and hence the surname of " Harrow " commonly given them instead of Taylor.

Willie Harrow was in the practice of buying old worn-out horses, and seldom gave more than five shillings as the purchase price of the animal, consequently little work could be expected of such quadrupeds. One day Willie was driving a load of flax up Castle Street, and the horse appeared quite unable to draw the load. Willie applied the usual argument of the whip, but it had no effect, as the horse would not or could not proceed up the incline. In the midst of the administration of the punishment, however, a well-known clergyman, the incumbent of the Steeple Church, stepped forward to Willie and desired him to desist from cruelly beating the poor animal ; but Willie continued his infliction as if he did not hear. The clergyman repeated his order with louder voice and authoritative gesticulation, on which Willie turned his head slowly round, and hissed through his buck teeth, " Ye've nae business ; the horse is no ane o' your congregation." The bystanders laughed, and the clergyman, who was himself a jolly, humorous gentleman, joined in the laugh, and at his suggestion a few men went forward and, giving the cart a vigorous shove from behind, pushed the team to the High Street, which being level formed no obstacle to the further progress of Willie and his five-shilling steed. Some time after the above occurrence Willie had to send the horse to the knacker's yard, and was advised by his brothers Andrew and Tam to buy a country horse, and give a better price for it than the value of the skin, which Willie accordingly did,

a farmer in the neighbourhood having supplied Willie with
a sorrel nag at the price of ten shillings. Having got the
horse inside the house (Willie and his horse always inhabited
the same apartment, viz., a cellar in one of the closes between
Seagate and Murraygate), he procured a bag of sawdust,
of which he placed a portion in the horse's trough or manger,
apparently in expectation that the brute would make a meal
of it ; but instead of that the horse snorted through its nostrils
and blew the sawdust about the floor with evident contempt,
and turning to Willie, appeared as if to ask whether he saw
anything green in its flashing eye.   Willie put on one of his
droll looks, and twisting his features to the expression point,
remarked to his brother Andrew, who was looking on, " Wha
would have thocht that a country horse would have known
the difference between sawdust and bran ? " Willie Harrow,
as well as his horse, was for many years a household word
in Dundee, and so unique in his singularity was he considered
by the urchins whom he amused that their sense of his
unrivalled eccentricities was generally expressed by them
in the following juvenile attempt at rhyme :

" Willie Harrow,
Deil a marrow."

The family of Taylors were an exact duplicate of that part
of the population of Paris which French writers term *canaille*.
As a specimen of their social manners the following incident
will suffice.   Tam resolved to get married, and chose a female
from Lochee for his bride.   As in honour of the occasion,
he washed his face for once in his life till it shone as if anointed
with oil, and put on a black suit and white neckcloth, his
tout ensemble looking as ill fitted as that of a mute at a
funeral.   On the day appointed for the marriage the pair
proceeded to the house of the late Rev. Mr. Adamson, of St.
David's Established Church, where the ceremony was
proceeded with, and at that part of the service in which the
minister enquires whether the bridegroom takes the bride for
his married wife, Tam, instead of following the usual custom
of expressing consent by a polite bow, answered in the following
words, " To be sure I do, I just came here for that purpose."
The bride it would appear expected something different,
as in hearing these words she turned to the bridegroom
as if " scunnered " at his rudeness, and addressed to him the
following very expressive order, " Boo, ye brute."

Dying Address of Will Hara's Horse.

JAMES GOW

O Will ! O Will ! I greatly fear,
For thee or thine I'll toil nae mair ;
My bleeding back forbids to bear
   Your ne'er-greased cart :
Ilk joint o' me is e'en richt sair ;
   And sick's my heart.

Just as the clock struck twal yestreen,
I swarfed outricht, through fever keen.
Which made my twa time-blinded een
   Stan' in my head :
And think ere now I wad hae been
   Baith stiff and dead.

Ye needna' stan', and fidge, and claw,
And crack your whip, and me misca' ;
'Tis just as true's ye gie me straw
   Instead o' bran,
That my auld stumps forbid to chaw—
   I'll die ere lang.

Or, whan I couldna' eat the trash
Ye coft, whan ye were scarce o' cash,
Wi' hazel rung ye did me thrash,
   On head and hip ;
But sune I'll save ye a' that fash—
   Lay up your whip.

Gae, tell gleyed Pate, your wisest brither,
That Death on me had tied his tether ;
And syne come quickly, baith thegither,
   My corpse to manage,
And tak' me whare they took my mither—
   Staucht to the tannage.

But guidsake, tell na brither Tam,
That shapeless semblance o' a man
Wha's liker some ourang-outang
   Than human bein' :
Nor ane o' your horse-murdering gang,
   Your auld mare's deein'.

For a **WORTHIE** Job

**In Motor Vehicle Repairing
or Maintenance of any kind**

GET IN TOUCH WITH

The largest, busiest and most self-contained motor repair works in the district. Where Modern Principles of Specialisation have been skilfully and scientifically systematised, with the aid of the most up-to-date machinery and garage equipment, to the great benefit, both in time and money, of its many customers

Lamb's Garage

Limited

41 Trades Lane, Dundee

Sole District Agents for

AUSTIN

Cars and Commercial Vehicles

(whose dependability we strive to emulate)

Mak' haste now, Will, and gang awa',
For Pate and his auld naig, to draw
My pithless banes to Death's chill ha'—
    A dreary scene.
For ere you're back I'll lifeless fa'—
    Amen, Amen.

Titles of Dignity and Feathered Fowls

In Scotland the title of the highest subject of the monarch has always been pronounced in the same way as the domestic fowl with the web feet is in Scotland. In England it is pronounced duck, but in Scotland *duke* similar to the prefix of those holding the highest title of nobility. The story is well known of the Duke who appeared disappointed that a country urchin was not even civil enough to lift his hat, ultimately intimated that he was the Duke of Buccleuch, in expectation that the boy would at once fall down and worship the " breath of kings." Instead of this, however, the unconscionable little rebel quietly repeated the word " A *juke!* " and put the question, " Can you *sume?* " On being answered, " No ! " " Can you *flee?* " " No ! " The young naturalist intimated that his mither had a duke that could both " sume " and " flee."

Some years ago an interview of a similar nature took place between a late well-known otter-hunting Duke and a proprietor of an estate adjoining the Dean water in Strathmore. This gentleman, who was the descendant of a line of radical ancestors, and not famed for extraordinary delicacy in his expression, was walking one day along the edge of one of his fields, when he espied a man followed by a number of terrier dogs coming through the field from the direction of the water, and instead of selecting a path on the field edge was proceeding in a straight line through the centre. The proprietor at once hailed the intruder, and asked who gave him liberty to commit trespass on the turnip field. The stranger at once touched his hat, expressed his sorrow at having given offence, and in polite terms begged pardon. The proprietor retorted that he might have had sufficient sense to avoid treading down the young turnips, and at once ordered him off the ground. The stranger, with a blush on his countenance, intimated that he was the Duke of A——, on which the laird rejoined, " *You may be the drake of* —— for all I care, but

you shan't be permitted to trespass on my property more
than any other man." The Duke at once made for the
turnpike road without saying " good-bye," and the radical
landed proprietor was wont to laugh in his sleeve when he
heard that the Duke and his gillies were otter-hunting in his
neighbourhood in the hope that they would meet again, but
they always stopped short when nearing the polite laird's
property and gave it a wide berth.

Making sure of Future Favour

In the early portion of last century the traffic of the Tay
Ferries between Dundee and Newport was carried on by
open sailing boats named pinnaces, seats for passengers
being fitted up in the stern part of the vessel, the rig being
two large lugger sails. During stormy weather, and particularly when the wind came in strong and sudden blasts, the
navigation was very difficult, and sometimes disastrous to
the boatmen and passengers. Before the present substantial
piers were erected the pinnaces sometimes landed at
Woodhaven and sometimes at the old pier at
Newport, as circumstances would admit. On one occasion,
shortly after the pinnace left the Craig at the Dundee side
of the river, and when the vessel was about half across, the
wind, which at starting was rather fresh and gusty, resolved
into a complete hurricane, which made the pinnace swing
over to the lee side, causing the passengers to cling to the
seats or shrouds, while others were thrown down upon the
floor of the compartment. The boatmen shortened sail as
quickly as possible, and the vessel being less exposed to the
action of the wind, became more manageable, and ultimately
succeeded in landing the passengers at the pier of Woodhaven,
or what at that time went under the name of the " West
Water." Among the passengers on board was a cattle
drover, who generally went under the name of " Spitfire,"
a rather harum-scarum sort of chield. Spitfire had sent
on his man by way of Perth with a drove of cattle for the
Edinburgh market, intending himself to travel over Fife
and cross the Firth at Kinghorn. While the severest of the
gale lasted, and everyone in the pinnace was expecting the
vessel to capsize, this man was heard praying in Gaelic, and
apparently imploring that his life might be saved. What he did
say was of course not intelligible to all his fellow passengers ;

but one of them appeared to listen and pay great attention
to the Celtic utterances of the distressed drover. When the
passengers were landed at Woodhaven the gentleman who
had been listening so intently to the ejaculations of " Spitfire,"
went up to him and told him that he too was a Highlandman,
and understood the Gaelic language, and that he heard the
other at one time imploring God to spare him in life and the
next moment imploring the devil to help him in his extremity.
The drover looked somewhat ashamed ; and being sore
pressed to give a reason for his proceedings answered that the
only reason was that " she did not know whether the Deity
or the devil was to take her if she was drownded."

A Reverend Husband rebuking Domestic Extravagance

Early in last century, a preacher named Charles Whitefield
was Pastor of a congregation worshipping in the Tabernacle
in North Tay Street, now St. David's Parish Church. His
ministrations were somewhat of the cast of those described
as peculiar to the Rev. Thomas Weston, sometimes ridiculing
and sometimes anathematising the ways and follies of the
age ; and when there occurred a glaring instance of folly
on the part of his own helpmate he resolved to show his
impartiality by making that lady an example. At the time
above alluded to the style of dress assumed by the female
sex was equally provocative of depreciating remarks on the
part of their male friends as that at present in fashion. The
skirt was scant and short, but the style of the bonnet then
worn was of large dimensions, and the exact counterpart
of a coal-scuttle turned upside down. This head-dress
was composed of the most expensive material—viz. silk,
velvet, satin, or other expensive fabric, and the quantity
required to cover the foundation, with the ribbons, flowers,
feathers, &c., which formed the decorations, altogether
amounted to such a sum of money as no struggling head of
a family could afford to supply without either hard pinching
at home or accumulation of debt. Mr. Whitefield considered it his duty repeatedly to advert to the subject, and
endeavoured to turn into ridicule the attempts by impecunious
individuals to cope with their wealthy neighbours, and in
doing so he did not spare even members of his own family,
as the following incident proves :—The rev. preacher's
wife was very importunate for her husband to furnish her

with funds sufficient to procure a bonnet of the fashion of
the day ; but Charles, after explaining his utter inability
to comply with his spouse's request, respectfully declined
to enter into the transaction, and consequently imagined that
there was an end to the matter ; but he " calculated without
his host," not thinking of the truth of the saying that

> " Tis vain t' oppose the torrent of a woman's will,
>   For if she will, she will, you may depend on't ;
>   And if she won't, she won't, so there's an end on't."

It therefore occurred to her that she had at home a chest
of drawers with which she thought she might conveniently
dispense, and with the proceeds of the sale of which she
would procure her much desired bonnet ; and this she accordingly did, concluding that her *cara sposa* would not find it out.
The minister always had his weather eye open, and was not
long in learning the whole circumstances of the case, but
determined to keep quiet till Sunday. On that day, therefore,
he resolved to give a lecture on the vices and follies of the
day, and accordingly, in terms more plain than polite,
denounced the absurdities of female fashions, the misery
of families arising from the indulgence of extravagance
in dress, and concluded by the following allusion to the
transaction of his better-half in regard to her new bonnet
as she sat among the listeners to her husband's words :—
" And now Mrs. Charles Whitefield must walk to church
and seat herself among the humble worshippers of the great
Creator, with no less than a chest of drawers on her head,
a hitherto unheard of proceeding in the history of the Christian
Church."   The audience appeared surprised, and could not
solve the enigma ; but ere many days the key was found
to the riddle, and it is said that the *argumentum ad dominem*
conveyed by her husband's remarks was treasured up in her
mind, and proved as " good seed sown in good soil," which
brought forth fruit in the shape of more humble and less
expensive aspirations in her walk and conversation in after
life.

On another occasion Mr. Whitfield, like many others
whose labours mostly consist of addressing large audiences
from the pulpit or the platform, had often to submit to a
great deal of annoyance from thoughtless people, who appear
quite unconscious that the noises which they make in various
ways are exceedingly disagreeable and disheartening to the

speaker. It is strange, but true, that blowing the nose, and thereby drowning the voice of the lecturer as with a trumpet, does not seem to be considered by some people in the light of an impropriety, or as administering a shock to a refined nervous system ; but nothing is more likely to cause a complete breach of the thread of discourse than for some snuff-consuming and unconscionable hearer placing his pocket handkerchief to his proboscis, and with the whole force of his stentorian lungs blowing a blast like that which brought down the walls of Jericho. The speaker may, and generally does for a time stop his discourse and look daggers at the aggressor, while he coolly wipes his nose and returns his snuffy " wipe " to his pocket. But it is all of no use ; the offending party, relieved of the tickling of his prominent facial feature, settles himself down with the greatest self-complacency to listen to the resumed discourse, altogether ignorant of having been the means of giving the least annoyance. In like manner the *cacoethes* of coughing, although equally disagreeable to a public speaker, is indulged in *ore rotundo* by many who should have learned to suppress the disagreeable effects by the use of their handkerchief. The rev. gentleman did not mince matters when so disagreeably placed, without giving the offenders a practical lesson which they would be likely to remember on future occasions, as the following incident instructs :—On a certain occasion two rather swellish young men entered his place of meeting rather late, and the service had been already begun. These marched along the floor almost the whole length of the gallery, drowning the voice of the minister by the noise made by their boots upon the wooden floor. The preacher made a stop till the unconscious disturbers of the devotional peace arrived at their selected seats, and then uttered the following remark—" These young gentlemen appear to make more noise in the house of God with the heels of their boots than they do with their money in the collection plate."

Jean Lyall

A habitue of the Greenmarket about 60–80 years ago and of that class credited with being able to make a good living " from the dust made by the flying heels of the commercial man."

Locally, the residents of this quarter, immortalised by

James Grant in " The Yellow Frigate " were known as " Green ⁻ market Birds " and from thence sprang many a successful merchant and member of the professions. Many of the living will remember the massive building known as " Drummond Castle " with Fish Street on the North side and Butcher Row on the other. The subject of this article was an " Amazon " in build ; the writer remembers one incident of her displaying her phenomenal strength. A boy had fallen into Earl Grey Dock and on being " fished " out, Jean got him by the ankle in one hand and " skelped " his posterior vigorously with the other until the watery contents of his stomach were emitted.

A rude, but effective method of resuscitation.

Jean went round the numerous Fairs with her " sweetie stall " and at St. Andrews " Fair " she erected her wooden shop. The students, ever ready to play practical jokes, tied the foot of Jean's stall to a baker's van. The reader can visualise the scene when the van began to move and Jean's Herculean efforts to protect her property.

A wag of the period composed the following expressive couplet.

" Napoleon got the better of Josephine,
But was feart tae tackle Fuzzy Jean."

Pugilistic encounters were numerous in the Greenmarket in these days and when Jean's sympathies were aroused on behalf of the weaker contestant she boldly entered into the fracas and finished the fight.

In 1860 the property in which Jean resided was condemned and she was the last to leave the property, but not until the doors and windows were removed was she forcibly evicted by the police. In her last years she earned a precarious living by selling Dulse and Tangles in the Greenmarket.

Glass " Behind "

Readers will recognise in the word " Behind " a word to take the place of another vulgar, though expressive, term defining the posterior part of man's anatomy. The subject of this title, in the memory of those living 50–60 years ago, paraded very slowly along the Nethergate. He was of respectable parentage and suffered from pronounced hypochondria, having the delusion that his posterior, for some reason known only to himself, was encased in glass.

A well-known doctor of the time knowing that hypochondriacs do their best to nurse their malady and always appear to be most anxious to get rid of it, took an interest in this strange worthy and decided to try and effect a cure. One day the doctor called and finding his patient at home, ordered him to be seated for a medical examination. The patient definitely refused ; the doctor forcibly knocked him into a chair and at the moment of impact had arranged for his assistant to smash a pane of glass on the hearth stone. The patient fainted away and on recovery his brain became normal and the terrible impediment was for the last years of his life removed.

Wull Harrow

This worthy earned a living about 70 years ago by selling firewood and sawdust. In these days nearly every shop was heavily besprinkled with sawdust and Willie was able to earn a good living and also refresh the " inner man " frequently at the public houses from whence he derived a considerable portion of his trade. His supplies were obtained at the larger wood yards and his commercial instincts being developed, he arranged to take his sawdust at a price per bag. The bag he filled at the sawmill was an outsize. the one supplied to the customer much smaller.

The daily rounds were made with a horse—an old farm one and a good worker—and cart, and at the beginning of the day when Wull had paid for his stock-in-trade he was frequently left with a few coppers and would toss up a coin to see whether he would have a dram or the horse a feed.

On one occasion the coin indicated in favour of the horse and Wull addressed it thus : " Wid ye' like a feed ? " and no answer being forthcoming, Wull remarked, " Weel, as ye' winna answer, I'll hae a dram."

On another occasion Wull tried to bluff the horse by putting before it a bag of sawdust which it promptly nosed out of the way. " Wha' wid a' thocht a country bred idiot like you wad ken sawdust fae bran," spoke Wull.

The youngsters made great fun at Wull and timing their cry to a nicety would shout " What dae ye feed yer horse on ? " " Saw—dust and Fire—wud " cried Wull in reply.

Wull frequently made resolutions to refrain from drinking,

Equal to a fine liqueur

There are no two opinions about the whisky of which this is said; it is—

★ **Real Old Scotch**

WHITE HORSE WHISKY

All Classes of Jobbing carefully and promptly done
ESTIMATES GIVEN

JOHN HOSIE
SLATER
1a Urquhart Street
DUNDEE

All kinds of Slates and Tiles in stock
SMOKY CHIMNEYS A SPECIALITY

Telephone No. 5538　　*House Address:* 114 HAWKHILL, DUNDEE

and passing a few public houses, shouted " Weel done, guid resolution," but eventually he gave way and remarked " Come awa' in, guid resolution, and I'll treat ye."

Dirty Inker

Originally a solicitor's clerk, but fell on bad times and got occasional jobs at the harbour tallying jute and flax. Frequently earned a shilling or two clerking to Bissett, the Sheriff Officer, and his pseudonym was derived either from his doing his part in this unpopular vocation or from his evident hatred of soap and water.

Tempt the Ladies

A character who used to strut between Tay Street and Lindsay Street endeavouring to emulate a dude, without having the necessarily flashy clothing.

Stringie Jimmie

Reasonably well dressed but had a " renny " for collecting string from the ashpits and shop refuse awaiting the coming of the Scaffie's cart.

Fire Nanny

A big strong, stout, elderly woman who had a small shop in the Wellgate 70–80 years ago, who periodically partook of the " wine of the country " which brought out the loving disposition, and many a man, old and young, had to suffer the embrace of Nanny to the great amusement of the other pedestrians. She eventually reformed and lived to an old age, respected by all who knew her.

Forky Tailie

Sometimes known as Burn the Bibles, was a well-known character in the '80's of last century. The reason why he received these peculiar names is entirely lost unless the first was derived from his careless habit of allowing part of a garment to protrude from the seat of his pants, but it is more than likely that the name came from this character having appeared dressed in a cast-off " swallow-tailed " coat colloquially known as a " Claw Hammer " or " Forkie Taily."

Walking down the busier streets with a basket which no one ever knew what it contained or was for, Forky would suddenly stop, draw a large butcher's knife from his pocket and flourish it across his throat. He was never known to injure himself or any other person with this dangerous weapon.

Pussie Wally

An innocent old woman who conscientiously laboured for a laundry in Paton's Lane by pushing a large basket on wheels into which she put her collection of soiled linen. " Pussie " had a liberal supply of hair on her chin and with her otherwise peculiar looks was not unlike a cat. The youngsters took occasional delight in calling " Pussie Wally " and mewing like a cat to which the old buddy replied in a flow of unprintable language.

On her eastwards journey she made a practice of pulling up her vehicle at Cooper—the bakers, and was presented with a biscuit and called again on her return for a like pick-me-up.

Holy Willie

A religious maniac who paraded the streets 50 years ago. He was always, summer and winter, in a outsize grey overcoat and carried a Bible in his hand.

Without the slightest warning he would take hold of a lad or lass and with stern visage exclaim : " Ye're on the brink—Ye're on the brink."

Willie Aitken

A half witted character who earned a precarious living about 60 years ago, delivering messages for a wholesale ironmonger or other trader. He had a fox-like appearance and in many respects was more knave than fool.

Always hopeful of eliciting sympathy his replies were oft-times witty. Willie was asked if he had had his breakfast, " Om' I, the swe-lins o' the tea-pat."

One day on his rounds he noticed a display of bootlaces in a boot-maker's window with a large card " The Strongest lace in the Market, 2d. per pair." Entering the shop he

addressed the owner as follows : Mr. —— dae ye ken what
I'd dae if I'd tuppence ? "

" No, Willie, what wad ye dae ? "

" I buy a pair o' they laces."

Willie got his laces.

The Blind Fiddler

A worthy, " Hieland Donal " by name, who always wore
the tartan kilt on trews, time about. The breeks were always
well patched, especially at the " sit down upon." With them
he wore a short tartan jacket.

His wife was always with him and she carried a bundle
of stockings she had knitted ; and as he played, and sang,
she made good use of her time selling the stockings. They
came down from the Highlands every summer ; this happened
from about 1854 to 1870.

" Charlie Harris "

An Englishman, who had a bad squint in one of his eyes'
and always wore earrings. He was at one time a clown in
Giles' show in Lindsay Street Quarry, and when he was on
the stage the ringmaster went after him with the whip and his
antics used to raise a laugh.

He afterwards had a place in the Greenmarket where he
sold ham and cheese and when crying his wares it used to
sound like " Good Jesus," " 'Am Jesus." After this he was
an auctioneer on his own account, and used to give out bills.

He finished up his career as a bellman. He lived in Thorter
Row, where he left property when he died. He was a thorough
decent sort and was ever ready to see the funny side of life.

George Workman

Geordie was a little man of enormous strength and had
abnormally large feet. The father of the correspondent
who gave the compiler of this book the information was the
man who made Geordie's boots. A special " last " had to be
made on which to build the footgear for Geordie.

He was the son of a Mrs. Workman—a widow—who kept
a public house and Geordie got many an opportunity of
exercising his " chucking out " ability. His extraordinary

muscular development was exercised in Kirklands woodyard. One day two of the managers thought fit to test Geordie's strength and sent him down to the Docks to bring up an outsize log of wood. The task completed, Geordie asked if they wanted the log carried to any other place and the managers smilingly replied, No !

Geordie, sensing that he had been sent on a fool's errand gripped the two managers and squeezed them until they cried out for mercy.

" Major " Balbirnie

A Meg Balbirnie of masculine appearance who, when the 93rd Highlanders were in the Barracks, Dundee, at the time of the Crimean War, used to don the uniform and impersonate the sentry whilst he was refreshing himself at the nearby hostelry.

Meg was greatly annoyed if her acquaintances addressed her by her christian name and peremptorily reminded them " Major Balbirnie, if you please."

Jimmie Knight—the Whaler

When a young man he was particularly anxious for a " life on the rolling sea " and importuned a skipper to sign him on for a voyage as an A.B.

When it came to Jimmie's turn at the wheel the Captain told him to steer straight for yon star.

About an hour afterwards the Captain with his expert ear correctly surmised that his ship was not ploughing the depth of water that it should be in, rushed on deck and sizing up the situation expressed himself in voluble sailor's language " Why the —— didn't ye steer for the star as I told you ? " to which Jimmie replied : " Och ! I lost yon star, but I found anither."

Jimmie up the Lum

One of the well-known chimney sweeps of 70 years ago who frequently washed the soot out of his throat with the 1d. ale compounded at the many small breweries in Dundee. He had large flat feet which pointed to almost opposite points of the compass.

One day when Jimmie was " in his cups " he looked down at his feet and soliloquized " Aye ! ye want tae gae up Barrack Street and you ye buffer want tae gae to Mid Kirk Stile. Ye're baith wrang. I want tae get hame, sae come awa' tae Thorter Row."

Jimmie Mowat

At the middle of last century Mowat carried on a good going shop for the selling of his locally famous home-made candies, whilst his wife was prosperous in producing millinery. Both did well for a time until the demon " Drink " used his clutches and both shops had to be closed. In his descent, Jimmie retained a modicum of gentlemanly instincts and whilst his wife did her best to look after the sweetie stall he earned a pittance by writing letters for the illiterate at 1d. to 2d. per time according to length.

Chip-ar-ow

A George McLaren who came from Glasgow in his early days and settled down in Lochee.

When the South African War broke out, Geordie joined up and went through the whole of that campaign to return to Lochee where his career started as a " worthy," after he had disposed of the money he had earned in war gratuity.

He was of stout build and stood at the street corners where the out of work assemble, and did good service as an unofficial enlisting officer in the Great War time by spinning yarns to the prospective field marshals.

When his audience started to " pull his leg " he used the word " Chip-ar-ow " which is an Indian word for " shut up," and from whence he derived his name. His ready wit and cheery disposition always brought him a " drink " which he always looked for and under its influence he was the source of laughter to everyone and when no more " payment " was forthcoming he stalked away with the parting word " Chip-ar-ow." He " passed over " in the Eastern Hospital within the last three years.

Tuppenny John

A big man who kept a little shop at Stannergate Point, immediately to the south of the oil cake works which was a rendezvous of young and old 50–60 years ago. John, apart from the selling of Tuppenny beer, sold several concoctions of his own brewing, among these were Nettle-beer, Dandelion Ale and Brown Robin| and which with a sultana fruit cake appeased the appetite of his many customers. To this day the corner where stood the " shoppie " is known as Tuppenny John's Corner.

The Fish Cadgers

A class of itinerant street salesmen very common 40–50 years ago, and now to a great extent deprived of an honest living by the modern well-appointed fish shops all over the city. Scores of cadgers used to wheel their fish through the streets, many of whom were undoubtedly " Worthies " and had nicknames to suit their peculiar characteristics. Their " Cries " were sometimes musical but more often discord, and they invariably held a hand to their ears for some unknown purpose ; perhaps to protect the drums of their ears from the raucous shouting.

The older generation can recall " Caller—had—e—aiks," so many a penny ; " Caller—Here—in," and in the season " Sprats—Bawbee a lippie."

In weather unfavourable to deep sea fishing and hence no supplies, the cadgers paraded the streets with vegetables and fruit. " Bummin Ingins 1d. a pund, or twa pund for three ha-pence," was a regular supplier of large (" Bummin ") onions, whilst the cry of " Sweet Sev—ile orangers, nae foreign dirt here," was very common ; the taste of the fruit instead of being pleasing, would have brought tears to the eyes of the Sphinx.

When the fruit was saleable at the price of a copper the vendors usually shouted " Apples a pund, pears a half pund. Ripe Carse o' Gowrie piers, Honey piers and Jar—gan—ells."

Street Singers and Musicians

This class of entertainer was legion, but amongst the principal were : Jock Duff, gifted with a big voice earned a living singing on the streets, and frequently got engagements in public houses, &c.; his favourite song was " When Robin's gone to sleep wi' Mary." Jock, to win a wager, " togged " himself up and at a solemn part of a service in one of the parish churches broke out in song and was not only ejected, but landed in Bell Street, charged with a breach of the peace.

Jamie Burleigh another of the same type who illustrated his usual song " That's the time to catch them ; catch them in their prime " by disturbing the " feeders " on his person by " turning them on their backs."

Only two years ago, passed away a very popular street musician " Blind Jock " who in " fair weather and foul " could be seen in the Vault or near the Post Office.

Jock was an accomplished player on the piano accordeon and also a fair exponent on the fiddle.

At the football matches Jock made a harvest and usually played " Up wi' the bonnets of Bonnie Dundee " at the oncoming of the rival teams. At the finish of the game Jock's " eye-witness " account was marvellous ; he could go over the whole game as if he had had his full eyesight.

A contemporary of Blind Jock was Blind Mattie, also an accordeonist, possessed of good lungs but frequently singing " ditties " of such questionable language as to be unprintable, and her dancing was not of the type for a modern ballroom.

" Hoshie—poshie," who had a " kink " in his neck and lay his head on his right hand and sang the words of his name over and over again, varied by inane mutterings of an impossible type.

Darby and Joan

In the first decade of the present century, an old couple whose voices had suffered much by " war' o' th' wear " used to ellicit the sympathies of people by singing (?) well-known hymns, and those who listened attentively to the " asides " were entertained by many humorous expressions, not always in parliamentary language. One authentic specimen is given :

" I love Jesus, Yes ! I do.
(aside in rhythm)
Fat did he gie ye in the noo ?
Only a bawbee oo' oo' oo',
I love Jesus, Yes ! I do."

In the event of their receiving a silver coin, their voices rose fortissimo " Glory, Glory, Hallelujah."

G. FORBES JOHNSTON

Masonic Buildings,
BROUGHTY FERRY

CHEMIST

OPTICIAN

A modern pharmacy with Sight Testing Rooms attached. Sight Testing is carried out under the personal care of Mr. Douglas F. Millar, M.P.S., F.C.O.

In the season amateur photographers are given an unrivalled Developing and Printing Service. Films handed in by 10 a.m., ready 6 p.m. same day. Expert work is guaranteed.

G. FORBES JOHNSTON
Proprietor: **Douglas F. Millar, M.P.S., F.C.O.**
Chemist and Optician
148 & 154 Brook Street, Broughty Ferry   Telephone No. 7241

QUALITY SERVICE SATISFACTION

PURVEYORS OF HIGH-CLASS MEAT ONLY

If you place your Order with us by Telephone you will find an intelligent appreciation of your requirements at our end of the wire

ORDERS CALLED FOR AND DELIVERED DAILY

THE ABERDEENSHIRE MEAT CO.
LIMITED
28-30 WELLGATE, DUNDEE
Telephone No. 5337

REMINISCENCES

In the young days of the compiler of this book the outstanding " Shows " which his parents allowed him to visit were the Theatre with its annual Pantomime, leased by MacFarlane in Castle Street, where Lawley's Ltd., now have their china and crystal emporium ; the two well-known Circuses, John Henry Cookes and his talented family and Newsome with his favourite clown " Little Meers " ; Hamilton's Diorama with Claud Howell as conductor ; McLeod's Waxwork in Lindsay Street Hall and the visit of the Kennedy family in Scottish Song and Story. Of Sunday entertainment there was none and woe betide the " younker " who was found "peeping " out to the street from behind the closely drawn blinds. The only literature permitted was strictly of a religious type, although much liberty was taken to read surreptitiously the adventures of " Jack Harkaway " and " Ching, Ching."

MacFarlane had a secondary theatre at the foot of Castle Street in the building originally used as the Exchange Coffee House which eventually was bought by the Grocers' Benevolent Society and named " The City Assembly Rooms," then became the " Masonic Temple " and is now occupied by Messrs. David Winter & Son as a printing establishment.

Cookes Circus was a large wooden erection (built in 1877) immediately behind the Queen's Hotel, the entrance to the cheaper seats being the passage as at present serving the Palace Picture House (built 1892), the more expensive seats having entrance by a long red baized covered gangway entering from the westmost shop of the Queen's Hotel.

Newsome's Circus, originally in East Dock Street, was transferred to Craig Street after the filling in of the northern part of Craig Pier and the writer recalls the slipway into the water where the carters used to wash their horses and where " Betty Blair " scraped and washed the bellies of tripe for her well-known business at the foot of Coutties Wynd. The " Shows " of a secondary class were held in the Lindsay Street Quarry immediately behind St. Paul's Mission Hall in the Overgate, at the then vacant spaces of ground in the Seagate where the Majestic Theatre is now, and also opposite, where Robertson's bonded stores are situated.

The names of the proprietors of these " lesser " shows, or " Gaffs " as they were termed 50 years ago were Swallow, Giles, Hicks, MacGivern, Clarks and John Young.

The price of admission to these " Gaffs " was a few pence and in extreme cases payment for admission was made in kind even to the acceptance of a " Jeely Jar." Much amusement was frequently evidenced by unrehearsed situations as for instance the programme boys' shouts of " Programmes 1d. each " or " Terts and Leeminade " at a silent, though tense part of the dramatic exhibition. The writer recalls a play " The Smuggler's Cave " with the Hero (Hicks) and " Tally Mug " the villain as principals. Near the end of the drama the " hero " (Hicks) with his sword jagged a small bladder full of cow or sheep blood and the villain, " Tally Mug," made a magnificent " Deid Fa' " so realistically that the " gods " demanded four encores before they were appeased. A story is told of John Young who on an occasion had to make the Deid Fa', and misjudging the distance between the footlights and the auditorium, fell into the orchestra stalls. Equal to the occasion, John sprang on to the stage and exclaimed : " I can't even lie or rest in my grave," and disappeared behind the curtain. The " property swords " were made of the " girds or hoops taken from whale oil barrels and had an unfortunate knack of bending at an inopportune moment ; the fair tresses of the leading lady was " Tow " from Baxter's or " Beasties " Mill, whilst the " side wing " scenery could serve for either a winter or a summer scene when placed with the tree roots up or down.

Outside these booths or " gaffs " the wifie with the basket of whelks did a roaring trade and a cup full of these succulent crustaceans could be had for a bawbee with a " preen free gratis and for nothing " ; the " plop-plop " of the empty shells was far more annoying to the supersensitive than the modern practice of rustling " caramel " papers. The wags in the audience took a delight in throwing the shells on to the stage and oft-times the management had to appeal to them to desist, as not only was the practice a source of great annoyance to the actors engaged in " mortal combat," but in many cases and ways destroyed the realism of the " Deid Fa.' "

Both Newsome's and Cookes' circuses were burned down, The site of Newsome's being built on by Taylor's coalsheds and the Flower Market (now one of the city garages), whilst a more stable building, " The Palace ", was erected behind the Queen's Hotel.

The ground whereon the " gaffs " were erected (Seagate) was afterwards occupied by Stratton's stables and a small brick theatre for MacGivern, and eventually the bonded warehouses of Messrs. John Robertson & Sons, Ltd., was built thereon.

The " Old Cattle Market " 50–60 years ago became the rendezvous of the smaller shows until the erection thereon of the first roller skating rink and switchback-railway by Mr. Alexander Stewart of Dundee and Wormit.

This place of entertainment was well patronised for a series of years until the erection on the site of a large corrugated iron variety theatre for the Livermore Bros. (about 45 years ago).

Reference must be made to the coming of " Sequah " (Mr. Hartley) to the Old Cattle Market in October–November 1888. " Sequah," who had compounded an oil " Sequah's Oil " and a " Prairie Flower " for internal consumption, of curative worth to those afflicted with muscular rheumatism or suchlike, paraded the streets in a magnificent gilded waggon drawn by six prancing horses, at the rear of which was a raised structure occupied by a large brass band, whilst he sat in the lower part dressed like an Indian Chief. On arrival at the " Market " Sequah began his duties by extracting troublesome teeth free of charge, and at which he was admitted by practitioners as being an expert.

It was obvious that Sequah's band was trained to blow their instruments fortissimo at the moment of " grip " and extraction and so drown the yells of the poor victim.

The business part of the show then began by inviting " cripples " to be cured. " Sequah " was undoubtedly an expert masseur, as after half an hour under his hands the patient left the waggon in a sprightly fashion and the sales of the " Indian Oil " began.

At or about this time a sensation was caused by a well-known street porter, Gordon by name, undertaking to trundle his wheelbarrow to London and back and his progress was as keenly watched as are the sensational flights of Jim and Amy Mollison of this time.

Children paraded the streets lustily singing this refrain,

" Have you seen Gordon, the wheelbarrow man,
     On his way to London with his caravan."

F

Gordon succeeded in his effort, which was evidently a financially profitable one, and there were many copyists. Of the latter the most peculiar was McIntosh, the whaler, who lost both his legs by frost bite in the Arctic, completing the journey on his hand-propelled solid-tyred tricycle.

Reminiscences of these old show days would be incomplete without details of a great showman "Baron Zeigler" who occupied one of the circuses in the "off" season, for horsemanship. The "Baron" had many novel methods of attracting an audience to his variety entertainment, some of which were :—

A large "brake" was hired from Mr. David Stratton, Star Stables, Seagate, into which the "Baron's" company in fancy dress would seat themselves, drive off at 1.30 p.m., when the works had "scaled," and stop at the "George" public house in Castle Street. A large ewer of liquid refreshment would be handed to the "Baron" who would dispense the "elements" to his company whilst another section of the company would be engaged delivering bills descriptive of the wonders to be seen at the evening's show in Newsome's Circus. This was repeated at public houses in all the busy thoroughfares. Another method was for two of the company dressed up as convicts to jump from the "brake" and be pursued by another member of the company dressed as a policeman who "shanghied" the prisoners and replaced them in the conveyance.

At the evening entertainment every patron got a numbered ticket and at an interval in the programme the pompous and showy "Baron" would draw numbers from a hat corresponding with numbers attached to a very miscellaneous collection of articles displayed on the platform. Many of these prizes were suitable to the recipient, many were not ; as for instance the proud young lad who carried home a well-seasoned cheese being imperatively ordered to "Tak the d—— thing tae the yaird an' bury it."

Every Friday a Benefit Concert was held at which valuable (?) prizes were offered to prospective comedians, platform vocalists, melodion and other instrument experts, clog dancers, &c. The vocalist occasionally had to sing with either young pigs or ducks under each arm and the pandemonium was oft-times so hefty that the prizewinner of a set of china was left with only a saucer to take home. This was varied by "Hot Porridge" supping competitions at which the invariable winner was Geordie Tasker—the Hunchback who left the stage with his prize for having more porridge on his person than any other competitor. The greater quantity of porridge was on his " Hump." Of all the " Baron's " attractions the appearance of " Sir William Macgonagal " was the tit-bit. His appearance in full Highland costume was the start of a fusillade of all sorts of " ammunition "—bags of soot, flour, fruit in all stages of ripeness and decay and eggs of doubtful age, etc., etc.

To such an extent did this type of fun develop that the police authority stepped in and threatened the " Baron " with an annulment of his theatre licence.

The method adopted to separate the audience in the various priced seats was peculiar and consisted of tall iron railings resembling muchly the method of the lion tamers to-day in guarding the public from the activities of the Jungle representatives. The method of " Central " heating was an outsize primitive Coke-chaffer which was placed in the circus ring.

Among the star turns brought to the variety stage at about 40–50 years ago were Prince Bendon, the ventriloquist, who was also an expert cyclist and gave an exhibition during the day of hill climbing, &c. These were the days of the old high machine with solid tyres and his great strength was evidenced in successfully climbing Dens Brae, which feat was shortly afterwards emulated by the late Mr. John High, our fellow townsman. Then there were Rogers and Lundy with their popular song " Have you seen my Auntie ? " ; Pallas and Cusick ; Donigan and Grant ; Harry Lind singing his own composition " The Star o' Robbie Burns " ; Tom Berwick, the inimitable negro comedian ; Charlie Coburn ; Pat Bergin, the clever one-legged clog dancer ; Dan Leno ; Little Tich ; Marie Lloyd ; Vesta Tilly ; The Flying Dillons ; Little Una ; Bessy Arthur in character songs, her favourite " Dinna quarrel bairnies, try tae agree " ; The Savonas and Elliots, the Savonas being the first saxophone band to visit Dundee and the same company gave an outstanding exhibition of trick cycling under the name of the Elliots.

About 50 years ago Harry Lauder—now Sir Harry—made one of his first public appearances at one of these vaudeville entertainments he at that time being employed in Corsar's Mill, Arbroath.

Many of our readers will remember when it was *infra dig* for ladies to be uncovered in a place of entertainment and when the " picture " hat was a vogue, and how the " confection " blanked out the view of all spectators immediately behind. Polite requests for the removal of the obstruction having failed, more practical methods were adopted and many a " mode " had its beauty disturbed by a poke from a stick or umbrella.

The Fairs

Fifty years ago and more the Fairs were fixed date holidays and the only evidence of these remaining is the Feeing Markets.

Lady Mary's Fair was the largest and most interesting of these holidays and was held on the High Street. A very miscellaneous collection of stalls were erected round the square and in adjoining streets on which were displayed all sorts of wares.

A worthy well worth remembering was the " Umbrella Man " who beneath an outsize gamp sold umbrellas at a most reasonable price and who, after orating on the many good qualities of his wares—the up-to-date handle, the specially non-tearing covering, the adaptability of the frame which could be blown inside-out without damage, the self-erecting spring frame, &c., &c., concluded with the following statement, " You may take it or leave it or go home without it, I won't take the ninety-ninth part of a farthing less than 2s. 6d."

In these days the wages of workers were small, no doles or pensions, and notwithstanding this the fun of the " Fair " equalled if not exceeded the varied pleasures of the present generation. A feed of roasted " tatties " or a " buster " of hot peas was relished then as much as the " fancy " cakes and coffee in the present palatial tea-rooms. The ecstasy of acquiring a " Sugar Hert," a handful of " Curly Murlies " or a bottle of " Treacle Ale " and a slab of " Ginger-bread " is impossible to describe, and the advent of " Palmer " with his confections at 1d. per quarter pound, and his " walking sticks " of red and white twisted " rock " is a memory to make the salivary organs active.

A correspondent of 83 years of age sends the following memories of mid 19th century of the Old Greenmarket salesmen :

I sometimes visited the Greenmarket when I was a boy and I well remember the Lemon and Kali Man who sold it at the price of a ha'penny the tumbler " or you can have it in the powder a penny an ounce, or two ounces for three ha'pence and a teaspoonful makes a large tumbler. It's called the real American Lemon and Kali because it was first imported from America."

Then there was a man who sold old books : " What have we here ? Why ! the Sermons of the Rev. John Smith, this volume contains 350 pages, double column, close reading, of the finest literature of the day. How much ? One shilling—9d.—8d. You can have it for 6d."

There was Banks the Auctioneer or Cheapjack. " Here is the finest Sheffield cutlery, guaranteed ; 2s. 6d. for one dozen knives and forks." After he had sold a few dozens. he told the buyers not to go away with that stuff, it was no use, and he bent over the blade of a knife, where it remained. " That's the kind," he said, " for cuttin' puddin' round the corner. Hand back those you have got and 1s. 6d. and I will give you good stuff." The purchasers got the same knives and forks—the bent one being a special one for demonstration purposes.

There was Robbie Salmond the gingerbread man from Kirkcaldy who took up his stance with his caravan on the site before the old post office was built, now the Courier and Advertiser's handsome offices.

He attracted a crowd of youngsters by throwing away a lot of farles, then he would get a hold of a wifie's bag, having sold her some. As he placed the larger cakes in her bag, he gave each cake a separate name. Like this, " Here's a book we can a' read, here's the family bible."

And in the memory of the compiler of this book the visits to the Greenmarket on Saturday night were not only very popular, but in a sense educative and intensely amusing. Who of that generation could forget the loquacious vendors of medicinal nostrums in pill, powder, block or liquid form who claimed for their specific " A cure all, for pains in the belly, or back or elsewhere," and offered, if the pills didn't effect a cure : " Bring them back and your money will be returned in full." These concoctions were usually composed of soap, sugar and a mild purgative, and manufactured in Tindal's Wynd, Castle Court or Greenmarket, and given high faluting names with a foreign flavour and said to be the discovery of the Ju-Ju's or other aboriginal race. The cheapjacks selling any article from " a needle to an anchor " got the crowd together by distributing notebooks, etc., and played on the credulity of the listeners by intimating that they didn't care two straws whether the people bought their goods or not, " They were philanthropists and in the pay of a very wealthy firm to advertise their goods." "They wouldn't deign to take the hard-earned cash of the working man." Oh! no! But they succeeded with the assistance of their " gees " (confederates) in palming off cheap " Brummingin " goods at a good profit.

Of a totally different type was Jim Gallacher, a well-known character with a kindly disposed nature, a " guid gift o' the gab," and a fund of mixed humour.

Jim, after he got an auctioneer's licence, paid for by a well wishing grocer in the " Market," sold anything marketable. Having collected a crowd by smashing a few cracked plates, cups and saucers, &c., he would begin to sell his goods. He would pose as a wealthy man and remark. " I could sign a cheque for a thousand pounds "—a long pause—" But would they cash it ? Would they H——" When selling chinaware he would often take his tea from out an unmentionable article and volunteer to secure any article that was not on his stance, at a few days notice, after " taking the correct measurement." Frequently Jim would get a stock of watches to sell—old and new with a proportion of unredeemed pledges. After a sale or sales was effected, Jim would frankly tell the purchaser " It will go when it's carried " or " It won't go long enough to allow you to time the boiling of an egg." Jim, who did his annual training in the Militia, would come to the " Market," cast off the King's uniform and do a big business before returning to the barracks.

At the horse sales Jim was always the favourite auctioneer and his ready wit ofttimes brought a sale when other sellers were without an audience.

When a poor lot of stock was forwarded Jim frequently warned the buyers to handle the " puir brute cannily and for God's sake no' tae lean against it." On one occasion a mere skeleton of a horse was in the ring and Jim remarked " This yin's been fed off ' hie'land girds ' " (barrel hoops). When " on the water waggon " Jim discoursed ably on the evils of drink and was the pleader for many a poor mortal who was threatened with free lodgings in Dewar's Temperance Hotel (Bell Street gaol) and paid bail money and fine for his acquaintances in trouble.

The " Market " was a live place in these days and those still living will recall the " galvanic " batteries with the dial for indicating the strength of the current a customer could stand, the buzzer to attract an audience and the contortions on hands and face of the victim as the power developed ;

Greatest Stock ever collected
of Books on Dundee—Forfarshire
(or Angus) and surrounding
Counties.

ALSO BOOKS ON EVERY CONCEIVABLE SUBJECT

FRANK RUSSELL

Bookseller (New & Second-hand)

26 Barrack Street   -   -   DUNDEE

Telephone 4984.

'Phone 3408.   Established 1854.

ALEX. MURDOCH

(Grandson and Successor to Alex. Murdoch).

FUNERAL DIRECTOR

69 PRINCES STREET

(Corner of Middle St.)

FUNERALS CAREFULLY CONDUCTED IN TOWN
OR COUNTRY.   CREMATIONS ARRANGED.

CHARGES MODERATE

Every requisite kept in Stock

Special Selection of Wreaths, Crosses, Tablets, etc.

NIGHT ATTENDANCE

House Address: **50 Kenilworth Avenue, Taybank.**

the pawky little man with the " Test your strength machine "
with beautifully polished dial ; the " Punching Pad " and
indicator which showed what a human could get from the
striker if in an angry mood ; the " Striker " or " Hammer "
or " Try your strength," with its long rack to show how
many feet up the towering erection you could knock the iron
block and if successful in reaching the top and ringing the bell
another effort was given gratis ; the stands with the " Dollies "
at three shots a penny and a cigar (?) or a " monkey " every
time you succeeded in knocking over one of the heads ; the
coconuts, half embedded in sawdust which, if the player
succeeded in knocking off their pedestal became their prize ;
" Love in a tub," where a winner got a coconut
if successful in putting a ball in a tub or bucket ;
the airguns with slugs and darts ; the football shooting
rinks ; the " marble and the girn " with a prize of 3d. if you
succeeded in leaving the " bool " in the girn (customers soon
got so expert that this game died a natural death) ; " Jock
on the Clay " a game " agin the law " but usually played
behind a booth or stall. On a lump of soft clay, three inches
or thereby in diameter, a wooden pin or spile of about six
inches was placed, a threepenny piece balanced on top
which the player had to knock off at a distance of a few feet
with a knitting needle. If the coin landed on the clay, which
it usually did, your money was forfeit, but 3d. or 6d. was
paid if you succeeded in landing the coin outwith.

Space precludes more than a cursory reminder of the
many " side " shows of 50 years or so ago. Regular visits
of the " Fat Lady " ; handless man who wrote legibly
with his toes ; the boxing booths of Jim Stewart and others ;
the Marionettes ; the Boxing Kangaroo in which a well-known
lady donned the gloves ; " Professor " Cottrill who performed
marvellous aquatic feats among which was eating, smoking
and sleeping under the water and the outstanding item of
60 or 70 shillings being thrown into the tank which
the " Professor " retrieved with his mouth. On one occasion
he disgorged over £3 in shillings after he came to the surface.
The bicycle " round about " composed of old iron shod
" boneshakers " on a circular track which were driven not
by the modern method of steam but by hard pedalling of the
athletes.

The compiler remembers an incident at Forfar Fair where
the members of the Dundee Cycling Club headed by Father
Lawson mounted the machines and kept pedalling away, long

F*

after the 1d. time was up, greatly to the disadvantage of the owner. Exhaustion was the means of stoppage.

Jenkins, the Punch and Judy showman deserves a few lines. Jenkins—a Dundee man—has never been excelled at the use of the " Squeaker " and always got a sympathetic audience, especially at the part of the play where Punch used his stick on Judy but when the same instrument was used against the policeman, round after round of appreciative applause was given. No dog was ever better trained to his part than " Tobbie " and the realism of the Gibbet scene was a memory never to be forgotten.

Jenkins, who was a strong active man, put in his drills with the Militia and always had his show available and oft-times got a good monetary return by giving a private exhibition to his officers and their friends.

Annual visits were made by Wombwell's Menagerie. Lord George Sanger with his talented " ring " artistes, the procession at midday being a feature of his visit, the magnificently groomed animals, the gilded waggons and beautiful tableaux including " Britannia " has never been equalled by succeeding showmen ; the one visit of Barnum & Bailey's (1899) circus and many others which space prevents reference to.

Tay Whale

Among the multitudinous entertainers who visited Dundee and district the coming of the Whale was one that earns a place in these reminiscences and is a memory brainily and nasely worthy of a few lines.

During the first week of December, 1883, this " denizen of the deep " known as a " hunchback whale " attracted by the schools of sprats, crossed the Bar of Tay and disported himself between Luckie Scap and the Tay Bridge.

At that time the whaling industry had its centre in Dundee and on the whale's arrival the whalers got their gear into working order. It was first harpooned on Friday, 7th December, 1883, and " showed face " frequently and gave a magnificent exhibition of its art on Sunday, 31st December, when the " Blubber Hunters " were at church. A story is told of the watchers having seen the whale aground in Invergowrie Bay and making haste in their boats were astounded to find their " prey " was the Gows o' Gowrie, which Thomas the Rhymer refers to in the following couplet.

" When the Gows o' Gowrie come to land,
The Day o' Judgement's near at hand."

The whale was harpooned again on the 1st January, 1884 and was captured in an exhausted condition on the 7th January, 1884 ; landed at Stonehaven on 9th January, 1884, and sold to Johnnie Woods on the 10th January, 1884, at £226 ; towed to Dundee Victoria Dock next day by the tug boat Excelsior and for a period exhibited behind Johnnie Woods' wooden house on wheels at the East end of Dock Street. An easterly wind in Dock Street gave a reminder of the whale which remains vividly in the writer's nostrils. The skeleton, after being treated by Professor Struthers of Aberdeen, found a resting place in Dundee Museum.

The excitement caused by the coming of the Tay Whale had scarcely died out when a large shark was captured in the North Sea and brought to the harbour by a trawler. Two prominent merchants in the Greenmarket at once bought the carcase, but as it in size did not compare with the whale they at once severed the shark in two, drew out the two sections, placed bags of sawdust between and covered with a tarpaulin all but the head and tail. Some " shark."

These reminiscences would be incomplete without reference to the sports of 40–60 years ago. The opening of the Victoria Athletic Grounds situated between Albert Street and Dura Street where Balmore Street is now, and to the south thereof, by that fine old " ped " Adam Marshall.

The Annual East of Scotland Meet at the Harps Football ground, with the procession of all types of cycles from Albert Square ; the coming of Ross of Glasgow with the first pneumatic-tyred machine, and the derisive cries of the youngsters : " Go on pudding," etc., etc. The handicapper had no idea of the value of the new tyres and Ross was put 6 yards behind scratch. The track being made up of cinders for the occasion, Ross had little difficulty in lapping his opponents. The principal entrants for the cycle races were drawn from the Dundee, Forfarshire and Albert Cycling Clubs, and included Jack Baird, Roan Deans, W. J. Lowson, &c.

After the filling in of the Stannergate came an up-to-date football pitch and racing track—Carolina Port—and many fine efforts can be recalled of Bob Vogt, McLaren, Jack Killacky, Alec Black, Willie Alexander, Sammie Martin and

Of your five senses, which is the most important ❓

SIGHT is more important than all your other senses put together. Therefore, eyes deserve the greatest possible amount of care, Do not strain them. If you have to make an effort to see clearly, or if you "squint," proper glasses will help you to see quite clearly without straining. And, if you have the glasses fitted with Safety Lenses, your eyes will be safe from flying chips of glass. It is far better to wear spectacles while your eyes are growing than not to wear glasses and spoil your eyes for future years. There are special types of spectacle frames for young people. You can see them by consulting

W. S. M. STRACHAN

Consulting Optician

161 HILLTOWN
DUNDEE

the flying visit of Osmond and the great American pedlar Zimmerman.

The football teams of this period were the Our Boys at West Craigie Park ; the Strathmore at Rollo's Pier ; East end at Pitkerro Park on the Old Asylum grounds ; the Harp at East Dock Street, and later the Wanderers at Morgan Park in Mains Loan.

The outstanding players in these days were :

Our Boys.—Butters, Forbes, Evans, Taylor, the Porters, etc., etc., and the enthusiastic John Cameron.

East End.—" Plumb " Longair, McHardy, Tosh, Spalding and the Proctors.

Strathmore.—Dick Striven, Will Dickson, Phillips, Davidson —the " Needle," Easton, Munro, Tam Gilruth, and Pennycook.

The Harp.—Peter Rock, Gilmartin, Black Mick, D'Arcy, Owen Phin, O'Kane and Murray.

The Wanderers.—Mudie—the " Paddock," Macgregor and Gloag.

Gymnastics, which had a great vogue 40 years ago, deserve mention. Those grand old sports " Father" Shurrock and Walter Macgregor come to memory. The opening of a first-class gymnasium in the Public Baths in December, 1883 ; firstly in the second-class pond and latterly in the third-class ; the formation of the Dundee Amateur Gymnastic Society— the " Dags " who in their first year, won the 2nd Shield against Liverpool Gymnastic Club (1st), and Warrington G. C. (3rd). The team that defeated Aberdeen by 6 points in the Drill Hall, Dundee, in the 1st round of the National Physical Society's 300 guinea shield competition was : G. G. Rogers ; H. Betsworth ; D. Crowe ; W. R. Smith ; D. Gemmell ; T. Small ; Wm. Phillips and G. M. Martin. A few years later the D.A.G.S. and the Dundee Physical Recreation Society (D.P.R.S.) combined and won the Shield.

Credit must be given to " Father " Shurrock, F. Clease, G. Rattray, O'Porto, Sandy Anderson, Sam Stewart and Jack Davidson for the perfection developed in these fine old days and to the enthusiastic interest of the Messrs. Bell of Belmont.

Boating on the Tay called out every fine evening hundreds of spectators to watch the products of the Marines' and Livies' in single scull, double scull and four oar contests.

Our Ex Lord Provost, Sir Wm. High was an able exponent and brought the first " outrigger " to the river.

Steamboats on the Tay

In the early years of the 19th century and prior to the advent of propulsion by steam and paddle wheel, the transport of passengers over the river Tay was by means of row boats or sailing pinnaces.

A sad calamity occurred in the summer of 1815 when a sailing pinnace was swamped, 18 passengers were drowned. This occurrence left a number of orphans totally unprovided for and an appeal to locals for assistance met with a ready response and brought into service that most beneficent institution " The Orphan Institution." Paddle wheel propulsion took the place of the more dangerous sailing method of conveyance and the opening of the new pier at Newport in 1823 began the era of safer passenger traffic on the Tay.

In the 70's of last century and onwards began the pleasure sailings on the Tay, other than the ferry services, and was carried on by a fleet of tug boats as opportunity provided between the towage of the magnificent fleet of " clippers " from Calcutta with jute, and of the sailing vessels from ports all over the world. The names of the leading tugs at this time were the *Renown, Excelsior, Commodore, Protector, Charles Dickens, Star of Tay, Iron King, Lass of Gowrie, Star of Gowrie ;* steered by Captains Dykes, Legge, Cowperwaithe, Edwards. At or about this time, vessels exclusively used for passenger traffic were brought to the Tay and daily excursions were made by the s.s. *Argyle* the *Hero* and the *Princess of Wales.* The last-named vessel had an interesting career.

The " forward " and " after " part of this vessel were originally the salved parts of the *Princess Alice* which was cut right in two in the River Thames on September 3rd, 1878, by the S.S. *Bywell Castle.* About 800 or 900 people, singing and dancing, were returning from Sheerness when suddenly, in the dusk, the *Bywell Castle* rammed the *Princess Alice* and cut clean through the paddle into the ship. In four minutes 700 men, women and children had gone with her.

After being fitted with a new amidships she got the name of *Princess of Wales* and sailed on the Tay for a season or two. The " *Princie* " had a large promenade deck aft, similar to the Clyde steamers, but with a load of passengers she had a nasty, if not fearsome, habit of swinging badly and the local owners thought fit to remove her top hamper, after which she was re-named the *Albion.*

After serving a few years she was sold to owners on the Welsh coast ; returned to the Tay as the *Shamrock* at the beginning of this century and was sold for service in the Solent.

In the 80's a fine paddle steamer, the *Scotia*, was built by Messrs. Gourlay, Bros., Dundee, for service on the Tay but was eventually sold, due to her cost being too heavy to return dividends to her owners.

At the beginning of this century the *Argyle* was sold to foreign owners and the *Thistle*, a twin screw vessel, was left with the up river traffic and at the end of a successful season was sold in 1902 to the British Admiralty for service at Haulbowline Naval Dockyard at Queenstown, Ireland.

The following year a second *Thistle*, a larger, faster and better appointed twin screw steamer than her predecessor began service on the Tay and had a successful two and a half years' work until sold to the Russian Admiralty for service on the Yenesei. Rival companies offered services for a number of years, the steamers being *Shamrock*, *Marchioness of Bute*, *Kinfames Castle*, *Slieve Bernagh*, *Carlyle*—this steamer of high speed and extremely shallow draft did great service at the relief of Kut in the Great War—and the *Alleyn*.

The favourite Captains on these steamers were Todd, Edwards, Morrison, Muir, Pert, and Yeaman.

War-time requirements took the majority of these steamers away from the river and eventually a small paddle steamer from the Humber, the *Cleopatra*, was the only transport for a few years ; she in 1931, was obliged through the severe competition of motor cars and charabancs, to give up the service. For over 20 years Captain Tares conducted a daily service between Dundee and Balmerino with small steamers named *Bonnie Dundee* and *Advance*.

Every summer season for the past thirty years much ink has been spilt by people who have no idea of the circumstances, relative to the improvement of steamboat services on the Tay. It is remarked frequently by visitors when they view the magnificent stretch of water at high tide and the beauteous variety of the hill and pastoral scenery surrounding the same, " Why don't you Dundonians develop this river and make regular sailings as are to be had on the Clyde." That this could be done, is an engineering possibility, but at an enormous cost. The Firth of Tay is tidal and sailing times would alter at least an hour every day. There are two or three points on the south banks between Dundee and Newburgh where steamers of shallow draft could make regular calls, but these

are at parts absolutely uninhabited and belong to proprietors
who refuse to grant permission to erect piers or jetties.   The
only type of vessel to navigate the Tay from Dundee to Perth
at any state of the tide is a stern-wheeler of about 10 inches
draft of water and as the Tay in the wider reaches can show a
very angry mood it is questionable if the Board of Trade would
licence such a vessel.   The North side of the Tay between
Dundee and Seggieden is impossible for river services.   The
coming of the motor car is the prime reason for the unprofitable
running of steamboats on our beautiful river and secondly,
the excessive duty on alcoholic beverages, the profit on
which, in bye-gone years, was the means of making ends
meet or leaving a meagre dividend to the shareholders or owners
of the steamers.

The Cabbies

The old horse vehicle, now entirely off the streets was,
before the advent of the tramways, and for some time after,
the only means of transport in the city.   Many of the older
inhabitants will recollect the stances in front of the City
Churches, High Street and Meadowside.   In summer, not
by any means an unpleasant occupation, but in winter's
blast was one of the worst.   These " cabbies " had a " shelter "
in Lindsay Street, but unless at meal times was no protection
from the elements, and heavy rain or snow brought a harvest
to those ready to ply the whip.   Poor souls ! how often has
the writer seen a row of cabbies flapping their hands across
their chests to encourage the blood to flow and the poor
gee-gees standing patiently on the cold, cold stance.   Withal
the " cabbies " were a happy company and every one was
known, not by his proper name, but by a nickname whose
derivation was usually some peculiarity in manner, figure
or a characteristic of his " steed."   A few of these nicknames
are Provost Haggart, Keek in the Pot, Jess, Cabbage,
Black Swan, The Racket, The Sodger, The Blue Leek, Torn
Stockings, Auld Gaiters, Young Gaiters, Puir Joe, Auld Hill,
Young Hill, The Waiter, The Joiner, The Kipper, The Lamp,
The Monk, Bowser, Lord Young, Sugar Boolie, The Baker,
Foondrum, The Tightener, Bob the Groom, Stupid Loon,
Broken Rock, The Whale, The Doctor, Hip-pooches, Jimmy
the Gum, The Snatcher, The Dreep, Corkey Boyle, Anxious
Johnnie, The Gouk, Habbering Wull, Dizzy Ritchie, &c.
Habbering Wull's horse had a white face and when a very
big funeral was in prospect, a liberal supply of lamp black was

applied so as to conform with the religious conventions of the time. Readers will remember the funeral hearse with its roof embellished with large flying " plumes " of ostrich feathers and the high-stepping Belgian horses with a miniature plume on their heads, but few will be aware of the method adopted relative to the flowing tails of the handsome steeds. Many of these magnificent appendages were natural, a few were false and were kept in stock by the ostler. These tails were attached to the stump of the horse and belted to the crupper for such a contretemps of having horses casting their tails during the last rites would never do.

Dizzy Ritchie was one of the last cabbies to take his stance and as his christian name implies, one of the humorous (?) characters who sat on the seat of the Old Growler.

Dizzy had a bad accident and was severely crippled, but nevertheless, down he came to the stables for his " yoke." The groom remarked " Dizzy, ye daft man, ye oucht to be bed." " In bed, na' na', what's the use o' a man ga'en tae his bed and him no' weel." The advent on the stances of the Hansom Cab caused perturbation in the breasts of the older fraternity and Dizzy, seeing the Master in his hansom, which was a novelty with canary-yellow wheels, polishing one of the lamps remarked : " Look at that silly man ! cleaning his hansom in his lamp."

Telephone 3750

Joseph Thomson
(DUNDEE, LTD.)

Painters & Decorators

47 South Tay Street
Dundee

BARRIE'S
STANDS
SUPREME

~ ~ ~ ~

TO-DAY——as it did 100 years ago——the preference for

BARRIE'S
LEMONADE

is mainly a matter of taste ——*Good Taste.*

~ ~ ~ ~

The Ideal Drink for the Home

~ ~ ~ ~

G. & P. BARRIE
LIMITED
DUNDEE & GLASGOW
Established 1830

OLD TIME GAMES

The Bools (Marbles)

One of the most popular games in the memory of those living at the end of last century and had many variants.

The marbles were of various sizes—the ordinary " bool " made of fired earthenware was usually about ¾ inch in diameter —the " Doe " was a larger marble of the same material, in size from 1½ to 3 inches diameter. The " Mappy " was a size between the " bool " and the " Doe " made of a finer earth, whilst the " Peever " was a miniature of the " Mappie " and usually had a crude design in colour on its exterior.

The most valued of all the marbles was the " Glessie," made, as its name implies, of clear glass with beautiful interior usually in strands of divers colours.

" The Ringey " was the favourite type of this game and proud was the boy with a new heel clamp on his boots who could make a perfect circle on the pavement by using the ball of his foot as a centre and scribing with his heel clamp. One " bool " was placed in the centre and others—their " Lakes "—to the number of players, on the periphery. Five or six yards from the " ringey " was scored or chalked the beginning mark, or " Tause " as it was called. Each contestant in turn tried to knock out a bool or bools and these became his property ; then, wherever the " Plunkers " (the bool played from the hand) landed, the player continued until the " ringey " was " skinned." " Skin the ringey."

The " Noup " or " Strandie " was played in the gutter way or strand and was simply an effort to hit your nearest opponents " bool " which if successful was awarded by receiving another " bool " but never, unless in extreme circumstances, " The Plunker."

The " Holie " as its name implies was an effort to place your " Plunker " in a hole made between the pavement and any wall or sometimes a hole made in spaces between the causeway stones.

A " span " or length between extended little finger and thumb was allowed as free.

" Hashie-Bashie " was played by each contestant placing a " bool " in a row against the wall and from " Tawse " trying to shift as many as possible in one throw.

" Knuckely "—whoever was " down " had to place his shut hand with knuckles towards the kerb-stone and his opponent had to hit the closed hand with his " plunker." If successful he got another trial, if unsuccessful he was " down." " Nae scunction " was allowed, inferring that the knuckles of the shooter had to remain on the edge of the kerb-stone when delivering his shot.

In all the " bool " games a peculiar expression was used " On your Chow " and the how or therefor of the derivation of the word is lost in the misty past. The meaning of " Chow " was when a boy was reduced to his last " bool " and lost, the boy with a surplus of ammunition good-heartedly offered to lend a " bool or bools " to allow the game to proceed.

" Fat-im in, Fat-im oot," was certain regulations referring to the " Ringie " but the compiler forgets and has failed to get a definition.

" A'thing at Fat-im " indicated that all rules and regulations were non-existent.

" The Mites "

This game, like the " bools " had many variants, but the more popular was the " Holie " and the " Ringy."

The usual " Mite " was the ordinary brass trouser button and many a garment was deprived of these most responsible adjuncts.

All " Mites " had to be made of brass, with the exception of one of wood called " A Banner " and allowed only in cases of extra " poverty." According to the weight of brass, a valuation was made ; a large button could be a " Twa Timey " " Three Timey," &c., the large buttons from the uniforms of soldiers, policemen, coachmen, &c., were known as " Flunkeys " and the sleeve and epaulet buttons from these garments " Half Flunkeys," whilst the most despised was the thin disc of brass covered with linen which got the descriptive name of " Shirter."

A necessary tool of the game was the " Nickem ", usually a flat stone or disc of metal about three inches in diameter. Happy was the boy who acquired a " Nickem " of lead.

The " Holie " began by making a small hole of about one inch between the pavement and the wall of a building, and from the edge of the pavement trying to throw the " Mites " into the cavity. The player who succeeded, retained his

" Mites." All " Mites " landing on the pavement became the property of the player who struck them with his " Nickem." .

The " Ringy " was a game similar to that of " bools." After the " ring " was scribed, the players stood at " tawse " and endeavoured to put the " Mites " into the ring. All " Mites " landing outside the ring were flicked in by finger and thumb. The player nearest the centre of the ring then tried to lift a " Mite " with the nail end of his thumb pressed down on top of it ; in the case of a large " flunky " the ball of the thumb at the palm end was used. A boy's collection of " Mites " was estimated in twos and called " Twecks."

" Knifie "

A game played with a knife with open blade on any grass plot and very popular in the many " parks " with which Dundee is favoured.

It began with each player qualifying by stabbing his knife in the ground ; then front " handie " and back " handie " as the name implies, the knife has to be dropped into the ground from the palm or back of hand. " Pointie " by gripping the tip of the blade and making the knife turn over and land in the ground. " Two pointie " by a double somersault, and " Pitch " by stabbing the knife in the ground and hitting it with the palm of the hand make it travel and find an upright position some distance away. Very often at this game a blade or blades would be broken, and a method of obtaining a sound weapon was tried by " Hoo' ye."

The broken knife was held in the shut fist with only the hinges showing and an effort made to exchange the useless knife for one of greater service.

The Sooker

A flat piece of leather with a piece of cord attached to the centre which, after being dipped in water was used to raise any flat object. An adaption of the Sooker was put to a more commercial use. A flat stone was tied to a piece of cord and soft clay, mud or more often stolen waggon grease, was put on the lower side. A thorough examination of the " cundies " under shop windows was made and any treasure trove lifted therefrom.

J. T. G. MILLAR

Hat & Cap Manufacturer
::   Gent's Outfitter   ::

59 MURRAYGATE
DUNDEE

J. T. MILLAR, Proprietor.   Telephone 3717.

COUGH CHLORODYNE

THE INSTANT COUGH STOPPER
Bottles, **1/3**

No. 1
HEADACHE POWDERS
10 - for - **6d.**

JAMES GREENHILL, M.P.S.
CENTRAL DRUG STORE
73 Overgate -   -   -   Dundee

" Bully Horn "

A most enjoyable game for a cold night and taken part in by both boys and girls.

" A " Goal " was selected, usually the cart entrance to a factory or wholesale trader's closed premises. After tossing for or mutually appointing a " goalie " the players scattered and hid themselves in some convenient spot easily accessible to the goal.

When the party were hid, one of their number would shout : " Bully Horn " and the goalie began his search. On " spying " a rival he named him and returned to the " Goal " and continued his search until all were spied. If, however, one of the " hiders " got to the goal first the game began again.

" Hoist the Flag " " In a Man "

A game similar to above but played by teams.

One team protected the base or goal whilst the other team went away and secreted themselves in the back alleys and pends, oft-times a considerable distance away. A spokesman from the outside party returned and gave leading directions, sometimes by word of mouth, but more often by indicating the path taken by the outside party to their lair, by using his hands. The lair was usually one having two exits. When either side " spotted " an opponent he shouted : " Hoist the Flag " or " In a Man " and sprinted either to protect the base or capture it.

Leap Frog

Played by a boy bending his back and placing his hands on his knees, the other leaping over the bowed back with legs astride. An elaboration of this exercise was :—

Lang Leeks

The boy bent as stated above, stood on an agreed mark and where the first leaper landed the " backie " took up his stance, the next trier had to leap from the " mark " over the " backie " and his furthest mark was taken as the new stance. The boy failing to manœuvre the leap was the next " backie."

Another game of similar sort was :—

Hackey—Duck

Sides were chosen and the side that was " down " bent
similarly to the above-mentioned games, but were all in a row
at right angles to a wall. One of the boys stood erect with
back against the wall and the first " backie " placed his head
against the first named who was called " The Pillow " or
" Bolster."   Many a " Pillow " was winded with the impact.
The first leaper got as far up the line of backs as possible,
the second and subsequent leapers following. If all the
leapers were successful they cried : " Hackey-Duck, Hackey-
Duck, Hackey-Duck, three times on and off again."

If the side failed to achieve their objective the other side
had an innings.

Dockey Aff and Dockey On

A strenuous and very dangerous game often finishing with
the players untamed, with bruises on all parts of their person.

A " Dockey " is a good-sized stone in the local vernacular.
One of the contestants known as the " Down " was selected
to guard the " block " which was a large stone which could
not be moved easily.

The " Down " placed his " docky " on the block and his
assailers tried to knock it off the block with their " dockies,"
and if they were successful in doing so, the " Down " had to
replace it and endeavour to " tig " (touch) some of his rivals
who in the interval again assailed the block.

If the " down " touched a boy whilst his " dockey " was
on, that boy became the " down."

A player was " untouchable " if he had his dockey in his
hand.

In the course of the game the vocal powers of the contestants
were exercised by shouting " Dockey Aff " or " Dockey On "
according to the position of the stone belonging to the " down."

Kick the Can

One of the " gang " was " down " and placed an old tin
can on one of the sewer covers—the " Block "—in the centre
of the street. One of the players kicked the can as far as he
possibly could and the others secreted themselves in any
manner of way. The " down " brought the can back and

replaced it on the block and proceeded to spy the other players. If he left his " block " too open a player could run over and kick the can off the " block " which the " down " had to replace before renewing his search ; if he " spied " a player and got back to the " block " without the can being removed the " spied " had to act as " down."

The " Boontry's "

This name is a corruption of Bourtree, Bower-tree, Bore-tree of the Elder species and having a soft pith was easily bored and made into a hollow cylinder. The earliest " Boontry " gun was made from this wood in a primitive form, but 50–60 years ago the boys found seasonal amusement with the " Boontry " of a more practical type, purchased from Sammy Lees or Dobson in the Overgate.

The modus operandi was having procured your " Boontry " with its fitted piston, ramrod or plunger, ammunition was the next requisite.

Corks were the favourite loading material but like all boys' accessories were either quickly lost or otherwise unavailable. Moistened tow and paper had often to serve the purpose.

At the muzzle-end was pressed the projectile and at the breech end was " thumped " in the " shell."

When the shell was entered it was forcibly pressed into the cylinder and out went the projectile with a loud pop. Recovering the projectile it then became the shell and so on and so on.

Chicky Mally, &c.

This in no sense could be called a game but was an annoyance to householders as a perusal of this brief explanation will show.

The boys having procured a " pirn " of thread, which as the reader can easily imagine was never purchased by them, proceeded to tie a nail or large button to a piece of thread 6 to 8 inches long which they attached to part of a window frame with a pin ; at the weighted end the rest of the " pirn " of thread was attached and from a " hidey hole " they pulled the nail or button with rhythmical " tap-tap-tap " on the glass of the window. If the blind of the window was pulled up they ceased work and began again when " all's quiet." To reach a high window the pin was replaced with a piece of soft clay or waggon grease and with an expert throw reached the different " storeys " of the building.

Tricks of this type were legion in the latter part of last century as instance : An old hat would be retrieved from one of the many open ash-pits and a convenient sized causeway block, brick, or large stone would be placed in the hat, which was then placed in an inviting part of the roadway or pavement. Woe betide the athlete aged from 6 to 60 years of age who tried his goal shooting abilities.   If a hat was not procurable, an old tin can served the same purpose.

Another amusement was to make up a neat parcel, if an old purse was not procurable, and place same on the pavement. An unsuspecting, though delighted " innocent," would come along and view his " find."   On stooping down to secure his prize it was whisked away from his grasp by a piece of string attached thereto, to the delight of his tormentors.

Sometimes the purse or neat parcel was left on the pathway with no string attachment and many a happy finder of a treasure trove would be disappointed on opening his parcel or purse to find it contained horse manure, etc., etc.

Other " amusements (?) " were tying the handles of the doors on opposite sides of the tenement houses, varied occasionally by attaching the handle of a door to the bell pull of the opposite door and then knocking on both doors.   The opening of a door rang the bell in the opposite house.   Tar, waggon grease and " dung " were sometimes placed on the handles of " low " doors and the coming of a resident was awaited with patience and joyous anticipation.   The young rascals would " keek " between the Venetian or linen blinds and see a happy family round the fireplace or in the act of enjoying a repast—a sharp tap on the window, smash went an old bottle, or other form of glass, on the window sill, up went the blind to estimate the damage and finding none, the domestic peace was restored.

Boys have always had a peculiar fascination for gun-powder and many a penny has gone into the coffers of Black, the ironmonger, in the Murraygate and when the necessary coin was not available the boys got a supply of unexhausted powder in the Lochee Road immediately after the old Time Gun was fired.   A miniature shower of powder came over the Barrack Park wall and the boys scrambled to retrieve it. The happy possessor of a cannon was a hero, but not to the excitable housewife at whose door it was fired.

If a cannon was not in the possession of the boys " Sputtering Doolys " were made.

These were made as follows—the gunpowder being in hand it was mixed with water or more frequently " spittle " and moulded into a cone. A match applied to the top of the cone set alight the damp powder and a cascade of sputtering fire was emitted. Many a door on the dark tenement stairs was opened to find the source of the pungent powder fumes which gathered on the stairway.

Another stairhead ploy of the young lads of this period was to mix Cayenne pepper with cotton wool and press the pad into a key-hole. A light was then applied to the wool and blown into flame.

The fumes with the vigorous blowing were wafted into the house with results that can be well imagined.

Pallaleys or Boxies

A game played by girls on the pavement.

Six to eight squares or oblongs were chalked on the pavement, or sometimes the setting of the stone slabs served the purpose, and the girls flicked a small flat stone, or metal disc when procurable, by standing on one leg and pushing it with their toe between the sections. If the disc landed on the lines or points they were finished.

Eenerty Feenerty

The team were arranged in line and the spokesman or woman chanted the following refrain at each word pointing to himself or herself firstly and then at a member of the party

> Eenerty, Feenerty, Ficherty, Feg ;
> Ell, Dell, Dome-in-, Egg ;
> Irky, Birky, Starry-rock ;
> Ann, Tan, Two's, Jock.

Whoever was pointed out at the last word came on the side of the chorister and so on until the game was finished. This was sometimes adopted as a method of finding a partner for other games.

Note.—With a little mental calculation the speaker could " Jock " any of his favourites.

Electrical Installation
of
Every Description

———

Phone 3388.

D. H. MORRIS & Co.
ELECTRICAL ENGINEERS
43 South Tay St., Dundee

DYNAMO
and
MOTOR
REPAIR
SPECIALISTS

Watch Your Windows "pull"
bigger results if you use BETTER
SHOW CARDS & PRICE TICKETS

The attractiveness of a Window
Display is enhanced and the
selling power greatly increased
by the judicious use of GOOD
Show Cards and Price Tickets.

TRY THE SPECIALISTS—
BRUCE & COPESTICK
THE DUNDEE TICKET WRITERS
COWGATE - - - DUNDEE

The Chuckies

A few pebbles were placed in the palm of the hand, thrown lightly in the air and caught on the back of the hand between the fingers and repeated until one failed to have any left. A variant of this and much more difficult was at the moment of casting the chuckies the player had to lift one or more chuckies from the ground.

Beesy

A modified form of cricket, played with a soft ball and the hand acting as bat. Teams were chosen and the ball thrown to the first man in.

If he succeeded in punching the ball he ran to a base marked on the wall and another player began. If he scored, he ran to the first mark which the previous player had vacated and so on. If a player punched the ball so far as to be well past the fielders he could " get a roondie off the tens " by running and touching all the appointed marks.

I Spy

One of the players covered up his eyes, or more frequently placed his head against a wall and counted ten, twenty or more. In the interval the others ran and hid in any likely corner.

The party who was in the " base " had then to endeavour to catch sight of the others, either by a full appearance, but more often by a distinctive feature on their clothing. In his search if he left his " base " and one of the others touched it first, he was " down again." If he succeeded in spying the others he was free and another was appointed to the " base."

Tig

A very active game played by both sexes and brought out many feints and jinks. One of the company was " down " and had to run round and try to touch any other contestant or any part of the person or clothing calling " Tig." The " touched " was then " down " and the game proceeded.

" High Tig " was played in similar fashion but if the boy or girl was able to get to some object higher than the ground as on the window sill or standing on a box, stone, or barrel he or she was " untigable." " Lame Tig " was as the name suggests, every player who was touched on any part of his person had to feign as if that part of his anatomy was injured, viz., if a leg was touched, he or she had to keep on hopping and so on with other limbs until all the players were crippled. " Touch Iron " was a variant, and no player could be " tigged " who was touching the iron standard of a lamp post, padlock of a door, a protruding nail or other iron object. When any player at Tig or similar games was " winded " he or she cried " A Barley " meaning a truce.

" A Dree, a Dree, I droopit it "

A parlour game but often played on the streets.

Indoors the players sat in a " ring " on the floor, but outdoors sat on their " Hunkerties " (coal miner fashion). The ring being formed, one of the players careered round the outside with a handkerchief in hand singing the following refrain :

> " A Dree, a Dree, I droopit it,
> A took a letter to my love
> And by the way a droopit it.

At the final words the handkerchief was dropped at the back of a player who had at once to grasp the handkerchief and try and " tig " the principal performer. If successful in doing so before the player reached, after much jinking, the vacated place in the " ring " he was free, but if not successful the game started again.

" Three times round goes our gallant ship "

A girls' game. They formed a ring by clasping the hand of a player on each side of them and careering round to the following verses :

> " Three times round goes our gallant ship
> And three times round goes she ;
> And three times goes our gallant ship,
> Until it sinks to the bottom of the sea."

All sit down on their heels—" Hunkerties "—they then sang the following :

> " Pull her up, pull her up,
> Cried the brave sailor boy ;
> Pull her up, pull her up, cried he   (All rise).
> Pull her up, pull her up,
> Cried the brave brave sailor boy,
> Until he sank to the bottom of the sea   (All down).

"Broken branches falling down"

Some of the players stood opposite each other in rows and held their hands to form an arch. The others marched beneath the arch as the following ditty was sung.

> "Broken branches falling down,
> Falling down, falling down ;
> Broken branches falling down,
> My fair lady."

Then as each player passed under the arch the words " Breakfast, Dinner, Tea, Supper, Nip her, Grip her " ; was said and she was touched on the shoulders at each word and clasped at " Grip her."

The player who was immediately under the arch formed by the two girls at the words " Grip her " was declared out and was asked whether she liked a red rose or a white rose. Making her selection she went behind the party indicated by the red or white rose and when all were out, a tug of war was the final settlement of the game.

"Initiation ? "

In almost all the trades initiating ceremonies were practised on the new apprentice and the Masters and foremen, who probably had been subjected to like treatment, were often parties to the fun.

The compiler, who was apprenticed to Messrs. Gourlay, Bros., engineers, was asked by a leading hand to go to the moulding shop for the " cubilie," on his way there he suddenly remembered that the " cubilie " was the furnace wherein at least 10 tons of metal was in a liquid state, ready for casting. Had he gone, no doubt the foreman of the moulding shop would have sent him to another big " shop " and so on. This method of sending the innocent round and round was practised in every variety of " rite."

Others were sent for the " half round ' square '," " the soft-pointed chisel," " the brass-faced file," etc., etc.

Mention may be made here of the summary way in which the boy who regularly " slept in " by being driven round the principal streets on a two-wheeled barrow with the illuminating sign " Not dead, but sleeping," or " The Sleeping Beauty," and frequently given a bath in one of the many horse troughs.

In the Dundee Harbour engineers' office the tyro was usually sent for the graving dock key.

One of Dundee Worthies—

SMITH, HOOD & Co., Ltd.

for COAL

With 73 years of experience

:   Service and Quality   :

48 Union Street, Dundee

Phone : 4071.

QUALITY - VALUE - SERVICE

All three are assured
when   dealing   with

W^M LOW & C^O L^{TD}

Scotland's Leading Grocers
and   Provision   Merchants

THE SHOPS THAT ARE TUNED UP TO
THE HIGHEST STANDARD OF EFFICIENCY

This was the large two manual key for the sluice gates and many a sore shoulder was made by carrying this tool which weighed at least a hundredweight.

The Baker's apprentice was sent for the " Crystal Chaffer " and after being sent from bakery to bakery he would get a flour bag with contents of a considerable weight to carry back to his new place of service and with full instructions to exercise great care as the chaffer was brittle and of great value.   With sore back he arrived " home," opened the bag, by instruction, and found a miscellaneous collection of old iron, bricks, etc.   In some cases the boy was sent for the " Crystal stabber for the funeral shortbread."

The " Hatters " had a similar errand for the young, unsuspecting apprentice but in their case the valuable accessory was the " Glass Iron for the hats."

The Painters' gag was to send the boy from shop to shop for the " Red strip for the barber's pole " or ordered to fetch a pot of " Striped paint."

The Jewellers had a standard practice of giving the apprentice a piece of metal to polish with Water of Ayr stone until " he smelt the smell of onions."

An apprentice to the Brushmakers was never fully " initiated " into the mysteries of his trade until he had either cut his hand with the trimming " Sweers " or burned his fingers in the " pitch pot."

The pitch used by Brushmakers is a fast setting composition used to fix the tufts of bristle or fibre in the wood or iron brush holder.

Sandy, the foreman, who was the proud possessor of a large and well-groomed beard was watching his chance to initiate a beginner at the trade.   Taking advantage of an opportunity he pushed the cautious boy's hand into the hot pitch.   Out came the hand and clutched Sandy's beard and the two were fast " united."   Sandy had that day to be shorn of his hirsute appendage and nothing riled him more than to be reminded of the incident by the question :   " Wha' trimmed ye're beard, Sandy ? "

The Plasterers usually sent the young innocent to a house where a new block cornice was being put in place, with a parcel which on being opened was found to contain an ordinary brick.

A budding Certified Accountant was sent to a firm of jute spinners for the Card Breaker and was politely shown a machine weighing at least 10 tons.

G

In other cases the " Innocent " was sent to other firms for the " Key for Judicial Factory " or to the several stationers for a " Bottle of Avizandum ink."

The Plumbers' first treatment of a boy was to alter his appearance with " Smudge " then to go post haste to a chemist with a piece of brass tube and ask him to vaccinate it.   When the boy was making progress and having seen the journeyman making a joint with ladle and wiping cloth, he was told to " try his hand " but always suffered by having handed to him a wiping cloth of well worn texture.   The hot lead did the rest.

The young compositor was usually told to get the two-wheeled barrow and go to a neighbouring printing establishment for a " Pearl Hair Space," and got the shock of his life when presented with a small piece of metal weighing the merest fraction of an ounce ; others were sent for the " Long Stand " and got it by wearily standing in the corridor innocently waiting for what was non-existent.

Bookbinders apprentices were sent from shop to shop for the Rough Calf Polisher.

Having read of Dundee Worthies let me introduce you to a Tailoring Service worthy of the name.

Tailoring at its best,
*   yet strictly moderate in price*

Whitfield & Sturrock
14 Cowgate, DUNDEE

H. H. WHITFIELD, Sole Partner,   Telephone 6281.

Dundee, (1815)

THOMAS HOOD.

" The town is ill-built, and is dirty beside,
For with water it's scantily, badly supplied
By wells, where the servants, in filling their pails,
Stand for hours, spreading scandal, and falsehood, and
tales.
And abounds so in smells that a stranger supposes
The people are very deficient in noses.
Their buildings, as though they'd been scanty of ground,
Are crammed into corners that cannot be found.
Or as though so ill-built and contrived they had been,
That the town was ashamed they should ever be seen.
And their rooted dislike and aversion to waste
Is suffer'd sometimes to encroach on their taste,
For beneath a Theatre or Chapel they'll pop
A saleroom, a warehouse, or mean little shop,
Whose windows, or rather no windows at all,
Are more like to so many holes in the wall,
And four churches together, with only one steeple,
Is an emblem quite apt of the thrift of the people.

.   .   .   .

" In walking one morning I came to the green,
Where the manner of washing in Scotland is seen ;
And I thought that it perhaps would amuse, should I
write
A description of what seemed a singular sight.
Here great bare-legged women were striding around,
And watering clothes that were laid on the ground.
While, on t'other hand, you the lasses might spy
In tubs, with their petticoats up to the thigh,
And, instead of their hands, washing thus with their
feet,
Which they often will do in the midst of the street.
Which appears quite indelicate—shocking, indeed,
To those ladies who come from the south of the Tweed !

.   .   .   .   .   .

" Like a fish out of water, you'll think me, my dear,
When our manner of living at present you hear.
Here, by ten in the morning our breakfast is done
When in town I ne'er think about rising till one ;
And at three, oh how vulgar, we sit down and dine,

Buy your Wines

and Liqueurs from

a Firm of Repute

NICOLL & PETER

**ITALIAN WAREHOUSEMEN
WINES & SPIRIT MERCHANTS**

16 Union Street

DUNDEE

Established 1820.   Telephone 3820.

And at six we take tea, and our supper at nine,
And then soberly go to our beds by eleven,
And as soberly rise the next morning by seven.
How unlike our great city of London, you'll say,
Where day's turned into night, and the night into day.
But indeed to these hours I'm obliged to attend,
There's so very few ways any leisure to spend,
For they ne'er play at cards, Commerce, Ombre, or Loo,
Though they often are carding of wool, it is true.
And instead of " pianys," Italian sonatas,
At their spinning wheels sitting, they whistle like carters.

   .   .   .   .   .

" A poor man who'd been reading the public events,
Amidst prices of stock, and consols, and per cents,
Observed Omnium, and anxious to know what it meant,
With the news in his hand to a Bailie he went,
For he thought the best way to obtain information
Was by asking at one of the wise corporation.
Mr. Bailie humm'd, ha'd, looked exceeding wise
And considered a while, taken thus by surprise,
Till at length the poor man, who impatient stood by,
Got this truly sagacious, laconic reply
' Omnium's just Omnium.'
Then returning at least just as wise as before,
He resolved to apply to a Bailie no more !

   .   .   .   .   .

" I have seen the Asylum they lately have made,
And approve of the plan, but indeed I'm afraid
If they send all the people of reason bereft
To this Bedlam, but few in the town will be left.
For their passions and drink are so terribly strong
That but few here retain all their faculties long.
And with shame I must own, that the females, I think,
Are in general somewhat addicted to drink !

   .   .   .   .   .

" Now I speak of divines ; in the churches I've been,
Of which four are together, and walls but between,
So as you sit in one, you may hear in the next,
When the clerk gives the psalm, or the priest gives
    the text.
With respect to their worship, with joy I must say
Their strict bigoted tenets are wearing away,
And each day moderation still stronger appears,

Morgan Tower

CIGAR EMPORIUM
133 NETHERGATE
DUNDEE

Weir's Special Mixtures
STRONG :: MEDIUM

Cigars and Cigarettes of best brands always in stock

ANN M. WEIR
Proprietrix.

Agents for Messrs. Wills ; John Cotton ; Carreras, etc.

Barrie's *Dispensing Chemist* -

Agent for Burrough's Wellcome & Co.
Park, Davis & Co.   Oppenheimer, etc.

Fine Drugs and Chemicals.
Serums. Vaccines. Local and General
Anæsthetics. Surgical Dressings

SPECIAL TERMS TO
MEDICAL STUDENTS

A. Y. BARRIE

Phone
4375 **Morgan Tower Pharmacy**
(Opposite Queen's Hotel)

Nor should I much wonder, if in a few years,
The loud notes of the organ the burthen should raise
Midst the chorus of voices, the homage, and praise.
For I cannot conceive for what cause they deny
The assistance of music, in raising on high
Our thanksgiving and psalms, as King David of old
Upon numberless instruments played, we are told ;
Nor to music can theme more sublime be e'er given,
Than of wafting the strains of the righteous to heaven.
They've a custom, a little surprising, I own,
And a practice I think found in Scotland alone ;
For in England for penance, in churchyards they stand
In a sheet, while a taper they hold in their hand ;
But here in the Church, if the parties think fit,
On a stool called the ' Cuttie,' for penance they sit,
And, as though absolution they thus did obtain,
Go and sin, then appear the next Sunday again !
Superstition as yet, though it's dying away,
On the minds of the vulgar holds powerful sway,
And on doors or on masts you may frequently view,
As defence against witchcraft, some horse's old shoe.
And the mariner's wife sees her child with alarm
Comb her hair in the glass, and predicts him some harm.
Tales of goblins and ghosts that alarmed such a one,
By tradition are handed from father to son,
And they oft will describe o'er their twopenny ale
Some poor ghost with no head, or grey mare without tail,
Or lean corpse in night-cap, all bloody and pale !

.   .   .   .

" Some large markets for cattle, or fairs, are held here,
On a moor near the town, about thrice in a year.
So I went to the last, found it full, to my thinking,
Of whisky and porter, of smoking and drinking.
But to picture the scene there presented, indeed
The bold pencil and touches of Hogarth would need.
Here you'd perhaps see a man upon quarrelling bent,
In short serpentine curves wheeling out of a tent,
(For at least so they call blankets raised upon poles,
Well enlightened and aired by the numerous holes),
Or some hobbling old wife, just as drunk as a sow,
Having spent all the money she got for her cow.
Perhaps some yet unsold, when the market has ceased,
You may then see a novelty, beast leading beast ! "

HALL

THE
Hall for a Happy Evening

Finest Oak Floor. Dining-room and Fully Appointed Kitchen

RETIRING ROOMS

Suitable for Private or Club Dances (40 couples), Marriages, Whist Drives (40 tables)

TABLES AND CARDS SUPPLIED FREE
USE OF PIANOS FREE

The Hall is beautifully decorated, heated and is absolutely free from draughts

REASONABLE TERMS

Apply : CARETAKER

INSTITUTE & CLUB
31 S. Tay Street, DUNDEE